LIBRARY OF AETHERS

ALASDAIR ROBERTS

Library of Aethers

SELECTED LYRICS 1994-2024

BOATWHISTLE BOOKS

First published in 2024
by Boatwhistle Books
22 Gloucester Road
Twickenham TW2 6NE
United Kingdom

www.boatwhistle.com

Reprinted September 2025

Text © Alasdair Roberts 2024
Foreword © Robin Robertson 2024
Illustrations © Annabel Wright 2024

Typeset by Boatwhistle in Bell and Albertus

ISBN 978-1-911052-09-8

Printed in the UK by 4edge of Hockley, Essex
on FSC-certified 80 gsm Munken Premium paper

For Annegret Blümmel, with love and gratitude

'There was never ane o' my sangs prentit till ye prentit them yoursel', an' ye hae spoilt them a'thegither. They war made for singing, an' no for reading; but ye hae broken the charm now, an' they'll never be sung mair. An' the worst thing of a', they're nouther right spell'd nor right setten' doun!'

Margaret Laidlaw's rebuke to Sir Walter Scott

Contents

Foreword by Robin Robertson   xiii
Preface   xv

Autumn   3
Ice Age   5
Seagulls, Belts   7
Exile   9
Tangled Hair   11
The Grey Havens   12
Well Lit Tonight (First Perthshire House Song)   13
Second Perthshire House Song   14
A Cataract in the Cavalry   15
Cyclone's Vernal Retreat   17
Hexen in the Anticyclone   19
The Last House   20
The Language in Things   22
I Went Hunting   24
Farewell Sorrow   26
The Whole House Is Singing   28
Come, My Darling Polly   30
I Fell in Love   32
Slowly Growing Old   34
The Evening Is Growing Dim   35
Hyperboreans   37
Riddle Me This   39
Waxwing   41
River Rhine   43
The Old Men of the Shells   45

Where Twines the Path 47
Firewater 49
The Calfless Cow 51
The Untrue Womb 52
Coral and Tar 54
Unyoked Oxen Turn 56
Hazel Forks 59
The Yarn Unraveller 62
The Flyting of Grief and Joy (Eternal Return) 64
So Bored Was I (Dark Triad) 67
Ned Ludd's Rant (For a World Rebarbarised) 69
Under No Enchantment (But My Own) 71
The Hidden Sin 74
The Sacred Nine and the Primal Horde 76
Haruspex of Paradox 79
Song Composed in December 82
The End of Breeding 85
The Merry Wake 88
Fusion of Horizons 91
The Laverock in the Blackthorn 93
Dighty Burn 95
Song of the Marvels 97
Peacock Strut 99
Plaint of Lapwing 101
Anankë 103
The Wronged Blacksmith 105
If There Is Any Light 108
Hurricane Brown 110
Honour Song 112
The Mossy Shrine 114
The Final Diviner 116
In Dispraise of Hunger 118
This Uneven Thing 120

Roomful of Relics 121
Child of the Elements 122
Pangs 124
The Downward Road 126
The Angry Laughing God 129
Wormwood and Gall 132
No Dawn Song 134
An Altar in the Glade 136
Vespers Chime 138
Scarce of Fishing 140
False Flesh 142
A Keen 144
Europe 146
The Evernew Tongue 148
Actors 150
The Stranger with the Scythe 152
Learning Is Eternal 154
The Tender Hour 156
Hymn of Welcome 157
The Green Chapel 160
Orison of Union 162
The Undiscovered Land 164
Lorica 166
The Auld Butcher's Apron 168
Remembrancer's Blues 169

Appendix 1: The Ruby in the Hawthorn 171
Appendix 2: Adeus à mágoa by Christopher Mack 175
Appendix 3: Rafe's Rap 177
Discography 183
Index of Titles and First Lines 185

Foreword

ROBIN ROBERTSON

When I heard *Farewell Sorrow*, twenty years ago, I was astonished. Here was the sensibility of Scottish ballads and poetry: the strange, keening edge to the voice, the lyrics' vulnerability in the face of love or horror or despair, the singing and playing of a young man channelling old spirits. Here – sudden as a manifestation – was a great songwriter, singer and guitarist: a musician with the word-hoard, the world-view, the timing and phrasing of a poet. I hadn't heard anything like it since Sandy Denny, Nick Drake or the Incredible String Band – except, perhaps, for the American musicians Will Oldham and Jason Molina – whom I learned, much later, that Ali not only knew, but had joined on stage and in the studio.

What I loved about that early album was the way the words and music were melded into a slow sureness, charged and charmed by myth or by history. In the title song, we are in the head of a Viking chief watching the ritual longship burial of his fellow warriors. The tune is stately, mesmeric, picked out on the strings of his father's guitar, the words grave and deliberate, the brilliant rhymes arriving like surprises but closing with that clinch of certainty, inevitability:

> And you can pray, pray and pray for Life
> But no, my friend, my dearest friend, please know this:
> That Life is but Death's own right-hand man
> In every piece of his own left-hand business

So arm in arm we'll run towards that pair
And we, as they, joined and double-threaded
And arms flung wide we'll run towards that pair
And never fear that which once we dreaded

I soon discovered that Alasdair was steeped, deeply, in British and Irish folk music, legend and folklore, and followed a pattern of alternating albums of traditional ballads with records of his own songs. It is often quite hard to tell the difference. In common with those borrowed from the oral tradition there is a haunted, almost eldritch quality to his compositions, which use the imagery, the vocabulary, the call and response, the sudden shift of register that you find in myths, fairy tales and Travellers' tales and which you hear in 'The Whole House is Singing', 'I Fell in Love' or the gorgeous 'Waxwing', for instance, or 'Dighty Burn', a more recent song, new to me, that was written for a short film.

Restlessly innovative, endlessly collaborative, while always returning to the lodestone – the otherworld of Celtic myth, the ballads, the *ceòl mòr*, the 'big music' of our islands – Alasdair Roberts is a guardian of the flame.

Preface

I've been making songs for about as long as I can remember – from the age of six or seven years, in the early eighties, vocally extemporising into a tape recorder to the accompaniment of a tiny Casio keyboard. Indeed, one of my earliest memories of the powerful sensation of mortification is connected with those early years of music making.

It must have been because of my interest in recording and music that I volunteered to make sound effects for the beginning of the school play (in which I also sang, but in a minor role since the main part invariably went to the more outgoing kid with the louder voice). I don't recall what these sound effects were – perhaps recordings of wind in the trees, or water flowing and gurgling, or rusty gates clanking. In any case, I recorded three or four minutes' worth of them onto a cassette, one onto which I'd previously intoned and plonked those early Casio extemporisations.

However, after recording the sound effects I forgot to scrub the rest of the tape clear – and the teacher forgot to pause it after those first three or four minutes had played through. So it came to pass that, to the laughter and jeering of my classmates, I sank red-faced into the ground as one of my Casio proto-songs blared loudly into the school hall, and my tender young soul was painfully exposed – for what felt like a lifetime but was probably only a matter of half a minute or so – before the teacher mercifully pressed the 'stop' button.

I'll never forget it.

On reflection, perhaps that's exactly what I needed by way of a formative experience – an inadvertent exposure to the kind of mass audience whose attention I'd now be happy to have! Maybe it's a big part of what led me to try to hone the craft of writing songs, pushing and pulling them into presentable shapes, to the point where now, decades later, I am just about comfortable enough to stand (or to sit, when in a less rock'n'roll mood) in front of people and reveal to them the workings of my mind and heart as translated into melodies, cadences, phrases and conceits.

Of course the songs of nowadays are more ... *conceited*. They're more veiled, coded, disguised than those of my Casio heyday, which were most definitely not designed for anybody else to hear. Yet despite the veiling and the coding, I've always strived for some true emotional core, some psychic or spiritual resonance, to each song, as I did when I was seven, eight years old (although I wouldn't have expressed it that way at the time!). In a sense, I have come, through the development of an individualised symbolic language (and perhaps paradoxically), to strive for communication through obfuscation, clarity through ambiguity.

The earliest lyric in this volume was written in 1994, when I was seventeen. Of course, there are earlier songs in the canon, stretching from those Casio songs – like nursery versions of the synthpop hits of the day – to raucous teenage creations aired in various high school bands, after my discovery of the electric guitar. For whatever reason, I considered it judicious to pass over all of those very early pieces when making the selection for the present book. Perhaps it's because, in spite of all the years that have passed since those childhood and adolescent days, I lack even yet the adequate maturity to live with the gauche echoes of those former voices. Maybe one day, however, if and when I've matured more comprehensively, I'll make my peace with them and there'll be a volume entitled *Juvenilia* to follow on from this one.

In a way I consider this selection as a kind of full stop on this particular phase of my writing career. It contains pieces spanning from my late teens to my mid-forties, presented more or less chronologically (I say more or less, because I didn't always keep precise records of when things happened). Hopefully this format allows the reader to observe the gradual stylistic progression (and occasional regression) of my work over the years; to recognise various phases, some discrete, others shading more subtly into one another; to trace persistent themes and preoccupations which might emerge, as well as more transitory, fleeting ones. A combination of gloomy musings and scribbled whimsies, let's say.

Finally, I would like to give thanks to the other contributors – to Annabel Wright for her wonderful illustrations, to Robin Robertson for his *conyach*, to Rafe Fitzpatrick for his *pwnco*, to Christopher Mack for his *saudade*, and to Màiri Morrison for her *brosnachadh*. And of course I would also like to give great thanks to Hamish Ironside for his diligence and enthusiasm as editor and guiding hand through the process of putting it all together. Perhaps if we're both still here in another three decades' time, there'll be a third volume, entitled *Senilia*, for the delectation of whomever is still buying books of song lyrics at that point in history.

Alasdair Roberts
Glasgow, February 2024

Library of Aethers

Autumn

You look as good
As I feel
I feel as good
As you look

Soil everywhere
A narcissus

Empty and long
Twelve o'clock
'Your winsome smile
Will protect'

No wood in the ground
No oxygen
No words in the air
Just hydrogen

Soil everywhere
Twelve o'clock
Soil everywhere
A narcissus

I had just started working in a Chinese restaurant in my home town of Callander in September 1994 when this song was written. I bought a Tascam Porta-07 four-track with the sum of my first few pay packets, and this was one of the first songs which I attempted to record thereon. In quiet periods at work I would scribble down ideas on the notepad which I used to take food orders. Some of this song's lyrics are based on a prognostication contained within a fortune cookie; it remains to be seen whether the import of that divinatory sweetmeat will be proved correct. The emotional core came from hearing, on a television documentary, Herbert Morrison's real-time eyewitness report for radio station WLS in Chicago of the tragic crash and conflagration of the airship Hindenburg *in 1937.*

Ice Age

Is it not about time that the stars aligned?
And is it not about time that the constellations slipped?
All the fishes swimming downhill
All the monsters slowly covered up in sand

Old Atlantis rears its head again
Stretches limbs to the pillars of the globe
And aliens in their UFOs
Flying over high Pacific fields

And what time do I have to love you?
I can't engage in a myth of such a size
Keep your cult and understand that
I'm not suggesting you should stay away from me

Until the ice age that has held me
In its clasp for more than thirteen years
Melts away and the equinoxes
Give a sign that the stars align our way

And it's a shame about the fallen arches
It's a shame about the fallen angels

Written in June 1995 and recorded the same month on the aforementioned four-track, this song was an attempt to fuse a reading of some crackpot apocalyptic theories regarding the lost wisdom of ancient civilisations, the precession of the equinoxes and so on, with contemporaneous, perhaps synchronous, personal experience. It was the first song on a cassette I gave to Will Oldham when he played with Palace at the long-gone Plaza Ballroom in Glasgow that same month. That encounter resulted in the release of the first Appendix Out single (featuring this song) on Palace Records in early 1996.

Seagulls, Belts

O, my girl of the old Armenian plain
Were you our cheerleader star of silent films?
You found a home in the oak's unrustled leaves
And from the timber you rose, from the forest crept

And when the pyre was built

And when the pyre was built I hid in the undergrowth
And only came to meet you when the others left
I know you saw the sunlight coming shakily
Tying Gordian knots around the prison bars

And when the pyre was built

Seagulls circle
Belts unbuckle

I flitted to the city of Glasgow in September 1995, at the age of eighteen, and this was one of the first songs to emerge that autumn after the relocation. I was attending a creative writing evening class at the University of Glasgow at the time, although I didn't share this lyric with fellow attendees. It is perhaps a manifestation of cianalas *and was the first song of mine to elicit tears in a listener. Let it stand that, in my youthful ignorance, I didn't know at the time that Armenia is in fact very mountainous.*

Exile

When you were on your Provincetown exile
A cenotaph was raised
A doleful folly sternly set
Against the sky
Against the sky
Against the sky at eventide

You left behind all the lakes and pines
And condescended to live here
They raised you well in that forest house
Then you came here
And you mingled your
You mingled your belongings with mine

Soon your warping bones will be
As gnarly as the trees they feed
Your spirit will escape aflame
Through the soil
Through the soil
Through the soil of the priory ground

Often the early songs are about trying to encapsulate or distil some ineffable and otherwise inexplicable feeling or mood; as such, it's difficult and possibly unhelpful to try to expand on them outside of the songs themselves. Nevertheless, I can say that song was written in Edinburgh in 1997 where I had amassed a collection of National Geographic *magazines from the sixties and seventies; at that time they would still turn up fairly often in charity shops. Many of the images within them were good for making collages, gig posters and so on. There was one particular photograph of an eastern church in the evening light which played a part in the eventual emergence of this song.*

Tangled Hair

In the frozen ground, turnips rot
In your old bedroom, an empty cot
On the windowsill, a broken pot
In the gloaming dark, a power cut

In your tangled hair, a bead of snow
In your coat wrapped tight, your body laid low
On a mountainside of blazing heather
Leave me not, leave me never

Leave me not
Leave me not
Leave me not
Leave me not

Several traditional songs feature 'impossibilia' – for example, apples growing on orange trees, the sun and the moon meeting in yon glen, fire turning to ice, seas raging and burning, and so on. In the case of this early song of mine, written in 1997 or 1998 and featured on the second Appendix Out LP, the impossibilia are simply root vegetables rotting in below-zero temperatures.

The Grey Havens

From the Norse air to the loam
Pulsing, breathing animals roam
Wisping ghosts in hidden lairs
Huge wings creaking in the air

Fog comes to the grey havens
Fog comes to the grey havens
Fog comes to the grey havens
Fog comes to the grey havens

From your tarry slumber pass
Tilt ye to the window glass
Vaulted prehistoric moon
Frosty stars are loosely tuned

Swan ships sail from the grey havens
Swan ships sail from the grey havens
Swan ships sail from the grey havens
Swan ships sail from the grey havens

This is another lyric for a song from the second Appendix Out LP. Written in my early twenties, it nevertheless clearly betrays the remnants of a teenage interest in the works of J. R. R. Tolkien.

Well Lit Tonight (First Perthshire House Song)

The bothy is well lit tonight
My friend has stoked a blazing fire
His brushes and his easel left
Abandoned by half-empty canvas

I teach to him the lore of years
And he shows to me a higher order
New the ceremonial home
We share a meal by hearth and candle

Strange the warmth I feel at times
When ley-lines run right through the middle
He gives the finest back massage
Upon the woollen rug we fumble

In my mind this is a clear companion piece to the following song: two very different houses hosting two very different encounters. First up, a bothy ballad with 'a wee threid o' blue'.

Second Perthshire House Song

A stranger rapped his staff upon my window
So I bade him come in dine with me that night
Cloaked and hooded, he gobbled up his soup

So I led him to my southern turret chamber
It's dank and mildewed, hay strewn on the floor
Gracelessly he sets himself in the cot

Then he's taken out his sword and swings it boldly
And creeps downstairs to where I sleeping lie
With one I waken, two I crawl and vie

I have a specific house in mind – grand and baronial, overlooking a loch in which I spent childhood summers swimming, hidden amid hills over which I once clambered. It's a house I've only ever entered in the clan feud of my imagination.

A Cataract in the Cavalry

Cities rarely disappear
From map to map
Babies rarely vanish
When you turn your back
Lineage rarely unwinds
From chart to chart
Kindred rarely severs
In the dark, in the dark
Fathers rarely weep so
At the word 'loss' hearing
And mothers condemn, justly
Forsaking their rearing

'I want to be a rider
Like my father
On a milk-white steed
A cataract in the cavalry'

This lyric, drawing on the legend of Kaspar Hauser, was written some time before I watched the great Werner Herzog's 1974 film Jeder für sich und Gott gegen alle *(known in English as* The Enigma of Kaspar Hauser*). I had first encountered and been fascinated by Kaspar's story in an encyclopaedia as a child. The first two lines of the final stanza are a crude rendering into English of the first utterance, in* Altbairisch *(Old Bavarian), that he was recorded to have made:* 'A söchtener Reuter möcht i wern, wie mein Voater gwen is'. *The artwork for the single on which this song was released,* Lieder für Kaspar Hauser *(Western Vinyl, 1999), was made by Annabel Wright, the illustrator of the present volume.*

Cyclone's Vernal Retreat

When the sun is out
Children sing in the vale
When the sky is grey
My soul is dark as a wake
Calmly we await
The cyclone's vernal retreat

Nestle together like birds
Close on a high bough

A runic legacy
In winter's skeletal leaves
That summer's axis feigns
Her bringing around again
For warmer weather's barbed
On autumn's bracken scars

Nestle together like birds
Close on a high bough
Under a sundering moon
Under the Great Plough

A rumination in two chords on the turning of the seasons, written in the spring of 1999. At the time there was a scheme whereby dole claimants could engage in certain projects in order to receive a little extra money every week; for my part, I undertook research into the history of Glasgow's Craigton Cemetery. This is how I came to spend a lot of time in the Mitchell Library, where this and the following song were written.

Hexen in the Anticyclone

The tides obey a lunar armoury
The winds command a polar certainty
Entwined, aligned barometrically
An Arctic trap, an impulse glacial

Beauty in the wayward growth of bones
And syntax used when speaking on the phone
Lairs uncoded, carved in sandstone
Hexing in the anticyclone

A counterfoil and companion piece to the previous song, again anchored in two chords. Neither song seems complete without the other, like the dark half and light half of the year. There is something in this of a visit to Castlerigg stone circle in Cumbria on a bright January day. Craigton Cemetery found its way in via the reference to lairs and sandstone in the second verse.

The Last House

O, where is my own true love taken?
Lieth she deep in greenwood slain
Or buried in some lonely drumlin
Or clay-cold in the raging main

The ivy has a sickly green pallor
Creeping not o'er the last house of her bones
The barrow-mound is guarded by phantoms
Whispering her name in the gloom

A crying ram I trapped in the barrow
A feeding ram does graze on the knoll
A dying ram I felled by an arrow
A bleating ram I chased round the wall

Her delicate bones are not resting
Stately in the tomb of a princess
Her lily-white bones are not facing
Westward with the bones of the damned

This song was written in 2000 and recorded the following year with Will Oldham and the late Jason Molina in rural Kentucky; it appeared on our trio record Amalgamated Sons of Rest. *Just outside Callander, by the banks of the River Leny, there's an old high-walled graveyard, an ancestral burial ground of Clan Buchanan. In my mind, this song is centred there. Its preponderance of stock ballad phrases indicates a fairly early dalliance with the song catalogue of the Mitchell Library; it's a sort of embryonic riff on the traditional song 'The Unquiet Grave.' Will referred to it as 'The Multi-Tasking Ram', so let that stand as an alternative title.*

The Language in Things

I feel the language in things
Within the littoral rocks
And in the figurative winds
Against celestial battlements

And in that ancient cursive scrawl
Materialising on the wall
And on the lips and tongues
Of our neglected young

Our elders' dislocated words
Distinct from what is overheard
The way that ciphers hide
Behind what is signified
Although all these things will fade
The words to describe them will remain

A rumination in two chords on the simultaneous and paradoxical materiality and immateriality of language. The second verse is indebted to Daniel 5:25. This was written in 2000 and recorded the following spring in a studio in East Kilbride along with Gareth Eggie on guitar and Tom Crossley on drums. I had recently acquired a bulbul tarang *and played it with a bow on the recording, to the distaste of the studio engineer who described its sound as 'horrible'. I learn now that the instrument's name translates literally from Hindi as 'waves of nightingales'.*

I Went Hunting

I went hunting in the morning, Polly
When the geese were in the field
I went hunting in the morning, Polly
The geese were in the field

And I saw a woman changing
From a woman to a gosling
And I saw a woman changing
Before my eyes

And the larks they sang melodious, Polly
At the dawning of the day
And they only know the one song
But they sing it wondrously

And the beauty of the singing
All along the valley ringing
And the beauty of the singing
Stayed my hand

This was written in the axial year of 2001 and seems to herald the termination of Appendix Out, the name under which I had theretofore made music. I was growing increasingly interested in traditional songs, in particular ballads ('muckle sangs'); this was an early attempt at writing a fictional narrative song.

Farewell Sorrow

Raise me high, raise me high
So I may see my fallen kindred seated
Who met with Death upon the battlefield
Who, in the end, fell and were defeated

And the way they were tricked by Death
Betrayed, betrayed, levelled and mistreated
I've stuck a knife in a man for less
But Death is not so easily defeated

And you can pray, pray and pray for Life
But no, my friend, my dearest friend, please know this.
That Life is but Death's own right-hand man
In every piece of his own left-hand business

So arm in arm we'll run towards those two
And we, as they, joined and double-threaded
And arm in arm we'll run towards that pair
And never fear that which once we dreaded

In the tenth century CE, the Arabic traveller Ahmad ibn Faḍlan journeyed to the banks of the River Volga in what is now Russia. There he encountered a people known as the Rūs, *or* Rūssiyyah, *probably Volga Vikings, and witnessed their longship burial ritual. Anthropologist Dr Timothy Taylor analysed ibn Faḍlan's written account of this encounter in his book* The Buried Soul: How Humans Invented Death, *which I read on its publication in 2002. This lyric emerged soon after. It is dedicated to the memory of Alan Thomas Roberts.*

The Whole House Is Singing

O, I know she rose early for I heard her sweet singing
Echoing over the flowering heath
She gathered the willow, the elder, the linden
The holly, the ivy twined into a wreath

'O, I long to possess them, the notes you are forming
They spring from your lips and ascend on the breeze
Had I risen early from bed in the morning
Then I would have hold of the notes you release'

Then she gave me the wreath and she sang like a starling
My fingers entwined in her feathery hair
But she shrugged me away and said, 'Alasdair, darling
When a song's on the wind it belongs to the air

'See: Polly, she sings as she sits at the spinning wheel
Mary, she sings as she skips with her rope
Johnny, he sings as he fetches the herring creel
Billy, he sings as he rolls down the slope'

The whole house is singing, the whole house is singing
The rafters are ringing, the timbers are thronged
The whole house is singing, the whole house is singing
And I overhear them, and this is their song:

We are stronger when the moon grows in the skies
And the moon causes the tides to rise and rise
And the weed carried upon the drawing foam
We will gather to bedeck our happy home

A pastourelle *and an early example of a meta-song. Perhaps it's inevitable that at least one song about song, or one song about singing, will emerge at some point in the canon of one who is engaged in the creation and delivery of songs.*

Come, My Darling Polly

Polly, you can tame the wild beasts
Your beauty, it can tame the wild beasts
Polly, you can tame the wild beasts
Your beauty, it can tame the wild beasts

Come, my darling Polly and be mine
Black olives and red wine
Come, my darling Polly and be mine
Black olives and red wine

Your body was my instrument of lust
Your body was my instrument of lust
Your body was my instrument of lust
Your body was my instrument of lust

My body was your instrument of lust
My body was your instrument of lust
My body was your instrument of lust
My body was your instrument of lust

You could not maintain your chastity
You could not maintain your chastity
No, you could not maintain your chastity
Even with the wearing of a girdle

You could never tame your lying tongue
You could never tame your lying tongue
No, you could never tame your lying tongue
Even with the wearing of a bridle

Come, my darling Polly and be mine
Black olives and red wine
Come, my darling Polly and be mine
Black olives and red wine

This song came very quickly and fully formed from the shadows, diabolical guitar tuning and all.

I Fell in Love

I fell in love with the roll of her drum
Fell in love with her horn's blaring noise
I fell in love with her lute's gentle strum
And I fell in love with her voice

Polly lay over so close to the wall
When I opened my mouth for to sing
My throat could not stall the melodious call
My words in the silence did ring

'I will squeeze your lungs like the bellows of an organ
And blow on your bones like the pipes
With a rat-a-tat-tat on your skull like a drum
A rat-a-tat-tat on your skull!

'I will fashion a bow of your yellow hair-o
For to scrape out a tune on your heart
Of your long fingernails I will fashion ten quills
For to pluck on your veins like a harp!'

Polly rose up when my words were all told
And this she did say unto me:
'I will visit the same upon thee thousandfold
I will visit the same upon thee

'May you become one with the waters so dumb
Flow away, flow away, flow away
Flow away, flow away, flow away, flow away
Flow away, flow away, flow away!'

One might, in an alternate universe, find this text under number 780 in the Aarne–Thompson–Uther Index: 'The Singing Bone'. It is inspired by defixiones *(curse tablets), beseeching the assistance of the syncretised Romano-British deity Sulis Minerva, which were cast into the sacred waters of Aquae Sulis (present-day Bath) around the fourth century CE. The specific tablet in question is one issued in retribution for the theft of a certain 'Vilbia', which might either be a personal name, or the term for a type of pointed tool.*

Slowly Growing Old

What are you doing, soldier bold?
Slowly growing old, slowly growing old
What are you doing, soldier bold?
Slowly growing old, said he

Of what is the world made, soldier bold?
Slowly growing old, slowly growing old
A little light and a little shade, don't you know?
Slowly growing old, said he

And how shall we measure it, soldier bold?
Slowly growing old, slowly growing old
By compass and astrolabe, don't you know?
Slowly growing old, said he

And what will you do when you are old?
Retire from this world of constant woe
What will you do when you are old?
Retire from this world
Let me go, let me go

To the memory of William Alfred Roberts, an old soldier, born and raised in Canning Town, London.

The Evening Is Growing Dim

The evening is growing dim
I know a place where we can swim
So leave your dress all on a stone
We're all alone, we're all alone

So fair of face and long of limb
So fair of face and long of limb

We undressed all in a glade
All among the gorse and bracken
And how my questing fingers made
Your every clasping to unfasten

So carefully, carelessly they strayed
Your every robing to unravel
Between your knee and your shoulder blade
They were unhindered in their travel

The gorse is growing on the hill
The crake is crowing in the bracken
Our limbs they lie together still
But in our slumber they will slacken

As magic knots evade all probing
Untangling only when it suits them
With fastness even in apartness
So too our bodies when they loosen

Like salmon writhing in the river
Diving with a final glimmer
So were the murmurings she made
As the evening grew dimmer

This song and the following one were both written several years before being satisfactorily realised in recorded form. Originally written around 2005, 'The Evening is Growing Dim' eventually featured on the Plaint of Lapwing *LP, which I recorded with James Green around 2013. Deep thanks to James for making the song work in a manner in which it hadn't previously done.*

Hyperboreans

Now the hinges of the year
Have rust on every rivet
The deeper we will have to breathe
The air just to outlive it
The more the sun shines in the door
Before the month of fevers
The more comes snow and so we know
Cruel Boreas deceives us
And if twelve o'clock I walk
A shadow's length behind you
The deeper I will have to dig
The driven snow to find you

Alas, alas, cruel Boreas!
You chill our very marrow
We will strew our pillow with
The rue and with the yarrow
When Boreas again begins
To blow a little harder
We'll go to our unwed bed
Therein to make our ardour
When Boreas at last relents
And the sun again is shining

We'll let the rhythm guide the sense
And the sense misguide the rhyming

O, we're the Hyperboreans
We dwell beyond the tundra
That's the name we glory in
And the name we labour under
If you would glory in a thing
It may as well be labour
That's ever been the reasoning
That governs our behaviour
The only way to overbrim
With love for every neighbour

Herodotus and other classical sources discuss Hyperborea, a land beyond the North Wind – to the far north yet blessed with temperate and agreeable climes. Some modern and contemporary commentators have argued that Hyperborea might be identified with the island of Great Britain, or perhaps the Isle of Lewis in the Outer Hebrides. This song imagines the inhabitants of that land, the Hyperboreans, as a relaxed, hospitable and well-balanced tribe. This song only really came alive a number of years after its emergence when shared by the voice and hands of Jackie Oates, to whom I offer deep thanks.

Riddle Me This

Show me the power that man cannot harness
To turn towards malice or work into woe
Be it the stars or the moon or the planets
Or the tide of the ocean in ever-encircling flow
Or everything under the ever-encircling sun

Riddle me, riddle me, riddle me this
Riddle me, riddle me, riddle me this

Who were the ones who first gathered the amber
To render the embering dawn of the day
The stallion in canter, the river in meander
So we'd remember them long after they pass away?

And how could they know as they measured the seasons
How could they know as they furrowed the soil
Of all the dishonour and all the unreason
And all of the wrong to be done in the name of their toil?

A briar of brawn and a forest of sinews
Will rise from the power they ploughed in the ground
And so in this way their dominion continues
Under the ever-encircling sun going down
So runs the burden of every song I've ever heard

APOCRYPHAL FINAL VERSE, TYPICALLY SUNG BY CHILDREN ONLY:

Go waken, go hasten the Guild of Stonemasons
The crafters and carpenters all in a row
We'll build a new Babel in Alba's grey gravel
We'll raise an Armada 'n' patrol auld Dalriada's shore

For those unknowable people of old who may have made innovations and advances in good faith, and with the most altruistic of motives, with no awareness of the ways in which future generations might build with maleficence on their endeavours. I was thinking also about the creation of pigments for use in paints through the grinding down of substances such as lapis lazuli, here fantastically reimagined as amber. Thanks to Marija Gimbutas for this, as for several other songs from the LP on which it features, The Amber Gatherers.

Waxwing

Waxwing, waxwing, what do you bring
From the frozen north?
Waxwing, waxwing, we've been waiting on you

'I bring the amber that I have gathered
On the northern seashore
For the hatchlings I have fathered for thee

'I've been underground where wyverns are bound
And where gold and jewels are found
These I hoarded under my berry-brown wing'

We have no need, no need of your amber
Likewise your gold and your jewels
There is no true beauty in things of no use

Waxwing, waxwing, my only asking
Tether the breezes so cruel
Keep my young well feathered and their bellies full

Waxwing, waxwing, what will you do
When your days of fathering are through
When at last grim Death comes a-knocking on you?

'I can do nothing but fly in the wake of my kin
So I will soar onward undaunted and die on the wing
I'll die in a canyon of echoes, you'll still hear me sing
But still I will give to you all the things I bring'

This song must have been written in the late spring or early summer of 2005, when the island of Great Britain welcomed more waxwings than usual, seeking food because of poor berry harvests in their usual haunts further north. With apologies to the Wyvern Bindery, which stood in Clerkenwell at the time of this song's creation but has now relocated.

River Rhine

Where does the River Rhine rise?
Where does the River Rhine rise?
Where does the River Rhine rise?
It rises in her eyes

When I look in her eyes
I see the River Rhine
I see the river widen
She sees the Clyde in mine

The elm, the elm, the spreading elm
The finest in the Rhineland realm
Gives so freely of her withy
Beyond the Scabbard of Priapus
How fiery and free the sap is
In the towering, towering, towering ashes

The ashes tower, elm-enshaded
And her lashes flay green-bladed
The trees decay, the trees decay and fall
On the margins of the Clyde
Running with the Rhine inside
And the Clyde inside the River Rhine
And so her eyes in mine

A happy confluence. 'The Scabbard of Priapus' (here somewhat audaciously rhymed with 'sap is') was my nickname for a certain conglomeration of trees visible from the road north to Glasgow from England.

The Old Men of the Shells

As I roved out one Shrovetide eve
Among the bramble and the cloudberry
It's there I heard a strange melody
Blowing over the northern sea
The song of the old men of the shells

The old men of the shells, my boys
The old men of the shells
I left the ones who love me well
To find my home in the heathery dell
And follow the old men of the shells

I made my bed so shallow
Among the marigold and marsh mallow
It's then I heard the old men say
'Why deny the sea her prey?
Come lie with the old men of the shells'

So deeper, deeper I found my home
Among the samphire, among the ocean foam
The curlew call my curfew bell
Leads me to my bed of pearl
To lie with the old men of the shells

And though the words they sang were few
They had the ring of something I true
I listened long and began to sing
The way the unfledged bird takes the wing
I sang with the old men of the shells

I cast around to find my tune
Thinking then to sing the song all alone
But wise words on a foolish tongue
Howsoever sweetly they be sung
They jangle like the brassy bells of hell
They'll never please the old men of the shells

This song borrows its title from an English translation of the Gaelic title of a piece of piobiareachd *music, 'Bodaich nan Sligean'. The particular* piobiareachd *in question is possibly related to the song 'An t-Slige Chreachain', which is, on one level, about old men drinking whisky from scallop shells. The cloudberry is in tribute to the Finnish friends with whom I had shared* leipäjuustoa ja lakkahilloa *shortly before the writing of the song.*

Where Twines the Path

Wheresoever twines the path, I will follow
Wherever twines the path, I will follow
And when the map and fact mismatch, I will burn the map
When map and fact mismatch, I'll disregard the map

Though the road be dark as clove and long as laurel
In tornadic Arkansas and Alabama
And I can only buckle in and watch in horror
And listen to our language lose its former grammar
Still I'll make no quarrel
I will make no quarrel

Whosoever draws my bath, I will wallow
Whoever draws my bath, I will wallow
And whensoever nods my head, I will go to bed
Whenever nods my head, I will go to bed

And dream of where the sows of England rut and snuffle
Where the summer truffles cluster in the hollow
Where the stags lock antlers and give joyous bellow
If the path should lead me there, I'll gladly follow
I will gladly follow
I will gladly follow

A song about coming to terms with culture shock, written in memory of a long musical tour of the United States in 2005 which was disrupted by a meeting with Rita in the Deep South.

Firewater

How can I ever know you?
How can I ever know you?
Or know your way of living
Until I know your way of dying?
And how will I remember
Until I taste the nectar of your ember?

Where is the firewater?
Tonight where is the firewater?

How can I ever know you?
How can I ever know you?
How can I know you full-grown
Until I've known you as a child?
How can I ever tame you
Until I know what makes you wild?

Dates are beaten to a paste
And laid within our databases
From that paste we make our mortar
Quickened with the firewater

Then of course we hew the granite
From the deep part of the planet
Sky above us, soil beneath us
We'll build our library of aethers

Where is the firewater?
Tonight where is the firewater?

It's in the library of aethers

I began writing this in Portugal in late 2005, after an encounter with the local aguardente. *Later the song came home to feature in a documentary about Scotch whisky,* The Amber Light, *by Adam Park and Dave Broom.*

The Calfless Cow

I must be going, no longer staying
O'er towering mountain I must now leave
No longer staying, no more love laying
On one who wearies of the very air she breathes

This morning early, my love, I heard a cow low
A lonely cow low on yonder hill
This morning early, my love, I heard a cow low
A calfless cow low for a hornless bull

A parting song.

The Untrue Womb

It's of an untrue womb I sing
Wherein I find my mother
The untrue womb where all the plagues
Of all the ages gather

I'm sailing on a ship at sea
Far away from fire
I'm staring at the midnight sea
And seeing only fire

It's an untrue womb where bloodlines end
Though every vein runs open
And none may leave the untrue womb
The hymen is unbroken

And only one born in the caul
Can leave the untrue womb
And he makes none to bear his pall
The bloodline goes with him

This is one of the few lyrics which appear to have materialised rather than to have been consciously 'written'. The titular untrue womb has various manifestations, one of which is the London Underground network; the song came shortly after a visit to that city of renown in the company of my mother. An alternative version of the first line of the final stanza: 'And only one born to the call'.

Coral and Tar

If I was a pine I would ooze tar and shine
   in the moonlight
Moths would all swarm but they'd do me no harm
And it's only for you I'd be shining
But I am no pine, I'm a man in my prime
And I'm pining

Come over, come over,
Come over, come over
'Cause it's been far too long since we saw in the dawn
With our lovers

If I were an oak, sure I'd creak and I'd croak
   like a bullfrog
My boughs they would break and fall into the lake
But you know that I break for you only
But I am no oak, I'm a man in the smoke
And I'm lonely

Well, I took to the drink as if seeking a bog
   to be mired in
To join with the pine and join with the oak
In their blood oath to choke up the garden

To harden the earth against any rebirth
To crowd out the fennel and sorrel
To keep the moon's beams
From embroidering your dreams
And making the tarry place coral

So join me in coral and join me in tar
Come over, come over,
Come over, come over
'Cause it's been far too long since we saw in the dawn
With our lovers

When you are young and can stay up all night. Thanks to Alex Neilson for 'embroidering', which replaced my original 'invading' to make this one of my most frequently sung songs.

Unyoked Oxen Turn

One year I ran and ran and ran
In the east and the south and the north and the west
And it's only when I finally came to rest
Did I realise I had no legs
So I picked up again and ran and ran

And everywhere I ran I did proclaim
'I'm no cripple, I'm not lame
No, I'm just looking for my legs
I'm just looking for my legs'

Through Christendom, through Araby
And all through higher Heathenry
Up the shale and down the scree
Wondering where those legs could be

And in the gallery so vast
Ambassadors were breaking fast
And when I asked, they looked aghast
They said, 'We're just looking for our legs'

And in the balcony so high
Men of avarice rushing by
And when I asked, they gave a sigh
They said, 'We're all looking for our legs'

And in the dining hall so long
The shackled harper sang her sorry song
And the stone-eared feasters sang along
They sang, 'We're just looking for our fucking legs'

So I picked up again and ran and ran
And ran and ran and ran and ran
And ran and ran and ran and ran
And ran and ran and ran and ran
And ran and ran and ran and ran

And then in a city in the north
I came to the foot of the High-Low Stair
Something gave a twinkle in my eye
And there stood a sage in the frosty air

And to this sage I did proclaim
'Look: I'm no cripple, I'm not lame
No, I'm just looking for my legs
Tell me, brother, have you seen my legs?'

Then the sage gave a wink as a sage should do
And just as he began to freeze
He said these words, and I tell you true:
'Forget your legs and find your knees!'

So I bent to the task and took to the air
Up and down the High-Low Stair
Cross the chasm, cross the schism
Like a moonbeam through a prism

Time to live as the unyoked oxen turn
Time to turn as the unyoked oxen live

Customarily, I introduce this song in concert as 'a dream vision song about the importance of flexibility'. Around the time of its emergence I had become very interested in the work of the late, great Scottish Traveller storyteller and singer Duncan Williamson, in particular a collection of his tales entitled A Thorn in the King's Foot. *I had been inspired by the way in which many of those stories unfold; the sense of something true having been stated, without the usual accompanying sense of having understood precisely what that truth might be. The notion of unyoked oxen turning is based on the phenomenon of* boustrophedon.

Hazel Forks

Because my face betrayed a smile
Because my smile betrayed my love
I went down to the hazel grove
And we'll all go down together

The hazel forked three ways in my hand
Three ways in my blood
Three ways in my mind

First became a flock of cranes
They danced away in a Troy-Town maze
Their shrieking frames made a chill refrain
And they made a name unknown to man

I will now reveal the name they made:
'The Asphodel and the Lily Red
The Daffodil has lost its head
A Bloom of Dread, a Bloom of Dread
The Newlywed and the Nearly Dead'
And they'll all go down together

Next one frowned and he went down
Then gave a laugh and forked up the path
And flew away forever

Next one cowered and drew away
Then sprung back into my face
Because my face betrayed a smile
Because my smile betrayed my love
I went down to the hazel grove
And we'll all go down together

Only one more task to tackle
Before we reach the final battle
Loose the Earl o' Hell's belt-buckle
Crumple down his trousers

Here's the gifts of the infant suitor:
A cask of ash and a flask of pewter
A map of the city of the future
And a clutch of empty browsers

Here's the dowry of the leper:
A walnut shell and a peck of pepper
And an alder spray to carve a quiver
For a gang of hazel dowsers

They dowsed themselves into a tangle
Called themselves a hazel bush
They snarled so sweet and incomplete
That they stole the heart of a little song thrush

Trifurcation. This song contains a punning reference to my family lineage. My paternal grandmother Margaret was of the McCall clan; in old Gaelic, hazel is coll *and its month begins in August, my birth month. The very final verse is a base contortion of one usually found as the very first verse of the traditional ballad 'The Gypsy Laddie' (Child 200).*

The Yarn Unraveller

Your family is haughty
And rightly so, yet wrongly lowly
No gold in store but a trove of lore
So right, so wrong and nearly holy

I would love to go along with you
I would love to be your fellow traveller
If that's not to be, then it's not to be
And instead I'll be your yarn unraveller

It is the wound unstaunchable
It is the healthy woman's ailing
It is the ship unlaunchable
And yet forever doomed to sailing

And also the harp of triple song:
Liberator, Lancer and Marauder
And also the axe of double blade
Cleaving in and in-between disorder

What sisterhood has joined together
No brother feud can ever sever

And when will you come back again
Will I see you on some future ocean?
Or roving in some former glen
Or just whenever you take the notion?

When weeping men and women break
And reassemble in a jumble
When the true pretender lose his throne
When the humble be proud and the proud be humble

Now Pastor Glass has passed away
And the sponges have absorbed the Aegean
I will hitch a ride on an endless wind
From what must be fled I will ever be fleeing

The 'axe of double blade' is the labrys, *an ancient Cretan symbol of matriarchy (and possibly etymologically related to 'labyrinth'). Liberator, Lancer and Marauder are three street names I noticed in one city I travelled through in western USA (I can't remember which) when on tour in 2008. This song is for the late, great Elizabeth Stewart and her aunt Lucy Stewart, Scottish Traveller ballad singers from Aberdeenshire.*

The Flyting of Grief and Joy (Eternal Return)

Well, it's eighteen years since the loud cicadas
Made us all abandon our imperilled shores
Such a ragged band of true crusaders
To join our father in the War of Wars

We came at last to the field of battle
Near the waters of the endless Lethe
We heard proud Joy make her sistrum rattle
Against the fearsome ranks of Grief

Then spoke Joy most grievously
'Abandon hope and follow me'
Responded Grief most joyfully
'Abandon hope and follow me'

Meantime we'll see three forests rise
And fall in mulch and rind-rust
We'll see the woodsmen turn and fly
And the Devil take the hindmost

I'll call upon my inmost scorn
To lay upon their babies
And you'll call on your opiate wand
To lay upon their ladies

We'll see three cities form and rise
And crumble down to fine dust
We'll see the burghers turn and fly
And the Devil take the hindmost

Half laid in the chamberlye
And abandoned in some gully
Half hung on the gallows high
For folly and vainglory

And I'll stand in the fallen masonry
And say my sermons seven
For all the penitents in hell
And the celebrants in heaven

And you'll kneel in the crowded marketplace
And draw your vast mandala
For Zoroaster and Mithras
Jehovah and Allah

A tithe of skin, a toll of bone
A bloody libel burning
In Jericho and Babylon
Eternally returning
Eternally returning
Eternally returning
Eternally returning
Eternally returning

Then Joy fell slowly out of focus
To meet with Grief in the Elysian Meres
From out her breast there grew a broken crocus
From Grief there grew a rosary of tears

They grew to form a swarm of hornets
They took the air and they swarmed as one
This one apported three fire-garnets
So sealed the rising of the unconquered sun

The title is an allusion to Hamish Henderson's song 'The Flyting of Life and Daith'. In that song the two speakers remain antithetical to the very end, while in this song of mine Grief and Joy finally merge together. 'Eternal Return' is used in the sense defined by Mircea Eliade in The Sacred and the Profane. *The concluding verse is indebted to the traditional song motif of the rose and briar, entwining to make a true lovers' knot, as found in the ballads 'Barbara Allen' and 'Lord Lovel'. As in a dream of the rood, the Dupplin Cross in all its syncretic glory loomed large in my mind throughout the creation of this song.*

So Bored Was I (Dark Triad)

Enthralled was I, so enthralled was I
As I walked the woods and the mountains high
As I walked the woods and the mountains high
All in the morning early

Then coming from an urn nearby
I heard the sound of a baby cry
I paused awhile and gazed inside
The cry was mine, the babe was I

I was bilious and saturnine
As I walked from shrine to wayside shrine
As I walked from shrine to wayside shrine
All in the noontime early

Then coming from an old mash tun
I heard the sound of a young man come
I paused awhile and gazed inside
The cum was mine, the man was I

So bored was I, so bored was I
I stifled yawns, I swallowed sighs
As I strode mid tombs and sarcophagi
All in the evening gloomy

Then coming from a broken throne
I heard the sound of an old man moan
I paused awhile and gazed upon
The man was me, the groan my own

Then they moaned and came and cried
And raised their voices in dark triad
Saying, 'The music of our tethered sphere
Is only silence failing
It's mere distraction, mere veneer
While we 'wait the great unveiling'

Quite a straightforward and humorous (in the ancient theoretical sense) wee song: the Three Ages of Man meet the three defining personality traits of psychopathy to ruminate on Cagean conceptions of the nature of 'silence' and the intentionality of sound.

Ned Ludd's Rant (For a World Rebarbarised)

I dreamed a dream and a scurvy dream
A very, very scurvy dream
I dreamed I was Ned Ludd last night
I was trying to put the world to rights
And find the unifying theme
A very, very scurvy dream

Saying, 'The cosmos is desacralised
Now the world must be rebarbarised
The cosmos is desacralised
The world must be rebarbarised
The world must be rebarbarised

'Long before this brazen age
This makeshift age of forays
We men took pride to stand beside
Our solitary glories
Ourselves alone, ourselves alone
'Gainst highwaymen and Tories
Ourselves alone, ourselves alone
'Gainst highwaymen and Tories

'Now the age has come to rust
We've seen the death of wonder

Now we rob graverobbers' graves
And redisplay the plunder
And we fill some dead composer's staves
With irony and thunder

'You aborters, you haters
You whores and fornicators
Prepare to be undone
Prepare to be undone
Prepare to be undone
Prepare to be undone

'That's only what this old guitar puts into my mouth'

Around about this time I was haunted by the notion of Kekulé's ouroboros dream as a metaphor for the myth of progress. A nocturnal vision of dancing molecules morphing into a snake eating its own tail guided him towards what for him was a great discovery, but what for others could be potentially destructive. Perhaps this is a song whose time has come.

Under No Enchantment (But My Own)

First thing she gave me:
Two sprays of old dog's mercury
Then I knew that this was serious
And it was Sirius
Who shone upon the road ahead
Though light of day was there to hear us

All too familiar, all too familiar
All too familiar
Those brindled hounds behind her heels
All too familiar, all too familiar
All too familiar
The things a road reversed reveals

Then she rolled away from me in her own cave of gold
And so sadly I saw her unfold and unfold
Then she turned her face to me and said with one look:
'The willow grows ever aslant of the brook
Regardless the shape and the heft of your book
I was a bee and I was alive
But my wings they were strong and they beat for the hive
And anything round me resembling a drone
Just a ricocheted residue of overtone'

And this she did say as she leapt o'er the stile:
'Bridges like this must entirely lack guile
It hinges on us, son, to find our own rust, son
So give up the gloom, just trust, just trust'

All this with one look
And man, was I spooked!
And woman, was I spooked!
And boy, was I spooked!
And girl, was I spooked!

That was true lunacy, that was true lunacy
That was true lunacy
Like none I'd ever known before
That was true lunacy, that was true lunacy
That was true lunacy
Like none I'd ever known before

Last thing she gave me:
One dewy sprig of rosemary
And half a compass
And so I left her, and there I left her

Under no enchantment
Under no enchantment but her own
Under no enchantment
Under no enchantment but my own

An empty-handed hunter
An empty-handed hunter coming home

This song is based on a visit I made to a friend on the west coast of Scotland (with a copy of Meg Bateman's Dunaire na Sracaire *under one arm and Maude Grieve's* Modern Herbal *under the other), the uncanny sensations experienced there and the magical thinking which they engendered.*

The Hidden Sin

The hidden sin is half forgiven
The hidden sin is half forgiven
When by sin the world is riven
All that's hidden is revealed

And the one from whom I kept my raking
From whom I crept when day was breaking
Upon her brow before awakening
I lay a last lamenting kiss

And it's robes of mourning all around her
And loanwords only will she sing
That's how the fickle fates have found her
In scapegoat's idyll languishing

Oh, the heartsease and the eyebright
Oh, the heartsease and the eyebright
Growing in the glade at twilight
Twined with myrtle scythed at dawn

And the one with whom I broke a bed-vow
Her head inclines to the piano
And there upon her neck so narrow
I lay a first fragmenting kiss

I'll give my earldom for a thraldom
I'll give my freedom for the kingdom
No more delight in open whoredom
I'll give my mantle for a pall

The hidden sin is half forgiven
The wishful self is rent and reeling
In the underworld of feeling
Divided selves will all be healed

'The hidden sin is half forgiven' is an aphorism which I first encountered in the work of the Scottish writer Willa Muir; however, I believe it ultimately derives from the work of Boccaccio, whose Decameron *I subsequently read and came to love. A version of this song featured in Luke Fowler's 2011 film* All Divided Selves, *about the Glaswegian anti-psychiatrist R. D. Laing.*

The Sacred Nine and the Primal Horde

Light the need-fire, o light the need-fire
O, light the need-fire and the flame of bale
With narrow tapers in the cold hands of the dying
Waxen candles in the warm hands of the hale

In the graveyard, down in the graveyard
As I stooped to drink the sacramental wine
All for to lay upon the wounds of our dear Saviour
I thought to gather up the sacred nine

Hollyhocks and hellebores
To lay upon his open sores
The dogwood and the briar-rose
To lay upon him in repose
The amaranth and tormentil
To speed his blood and see him heal
The centaury, the celandine
To lay upon his open shrine
And last of all the mistletoe
Bane of oak and Baldur's woe
With mastery of every foe
In whichsoever land he go

Strike the bray harp, o strike the bray harp
Strike the harp and let the wires breathe
Strike the harp and raise your tiny voices
In Homeric hymns to mitochondrial Eve

Gazing waveward and ever waveward
As I stood upon the sacramental shore
All for to crowd around the tomb of our dear saviour
I thought to gather up the primal horde

The chandler his tallow, the farmer his fallow
The cobbler his leather, the fletcher his feather
Taverners and hostellers, taverners and hostellers
Taverners and hostellers and everyone now lost to us

Singing: 'Sleeping lord, o sleeping lord
Father of the primal horde
Once adored, now ever more
Ever more forsaken
Must we too, o, must we too
Eventually lie down like you
On bed of rue and never more
Never more awaken?'

A song of metaphysical enquiry for F. Marian McNeill, whose The Silver Bough *I was reading around the time of its creation (and whose recipes elsewhere for Cullen skink and cranachan are very useful), along with translations of the Middle English York Mystery Plays (and, indeed, the Homeric Hymns). I am indebted to Ted Hughes for 'the sacred nine' and Sigmund Freud for 'the primal horde' and, of course, to William Taylor for the bray harp.*

Haruspex of Paradox

The fiend was reared in wonder-lock's embrace
'Mid all the crimes and vices of his race
Woe come to all on whom he shines his face
The fiend was feared from womb to tomb
Incanting malison drear and gloom
Woe come to all on whom he casts his rune

'I'm the son of many shifts
And I'm the son of boundlessness
And I'm the bird of loudest lay
I come to maim, I come to slay!
I'm the haruspex of paradox
And the oracle of double voice
You human wrecks, you have no choice
I come to cease the games you play!
I was here when time began
And I'll be here when time is gone
For I'm the howling son of dawn
Yes, I'm the howling son of dawn!'

He sang the hamadryad awake
With sharpened heel she three times marked the ground
And turned her thrice around, around, around
And sang a bonny song of flowing stave:

'Come, tell me who did me conceive?'
'Twas love
'Who weaned and nursed me and relieved?'
'Twas love
'Can love by love obtainèd be?'
By love
'Who gathers in the victory
But love?
Has stewardry of land and sea
But love?
What else explain the mystery
But love?
How may a man good works perform?'
By love
'And who can two to one transform but love?'

'But there is no love in his uncomely gloat
I would that it had died within his throat
He defames the ratios of the holy kirk
Damning every chancel, every nave
He was sent here to destroy the woman's work
To stay my bonny song of flowing stave

'So have him bound and stowed in cavern strong
Writhing with envenomed eye and fang
So mountains quake and gullies lash the land
Woe come to him who births a realm of sulphur
By his hand'

This song treats of the Norse trickster god Loki, and in particular the notion that his writhing when bound underground and bespattered with venom is the cause of earthquakes. I have encountered Loki most forcefully in Lee M. Hollander's 1962 translation of Lokasenna *('The Flyting of Loki') from* The Poetic Edda.

Song Composed in December

This song's made in anger, this song's made in love
Where the croak of the hawk meets the coo of the dove
Where minstrelsy's slander and rhyme turns to rage
To make a song about the ruination of the age

Woe to those who celebrate the taking up of violence
And woe to those who perpetrate delusions of their
    sire-lands
Who'd fight for no reason with sword or with firebrand
Be they reiver in the border or raider in the highland

And joy to those who celebrate
The breaking up of weapons
Who take a stand to raise a hand
Against oncoming slaughter
And joy to those who strive to give
A voice to those with none
The fosterer of errant son
And sire of wild daughter

And joy to those who'd use their songs
As clues to find their clan
But woe to those who'd use them
To enslave their fellow man

From open moor where kestrels soar on wings of beauty
To cloisters where vestals bear their palms of beauty
To waterfall tumbling, cascading and purling
To the flowery machair where the echo mocks the yellow yorlin

From forest deep where numens peep from every oaken bole
To city streets where people seek completion of the soul
For everyone with double bond of suffering to thole
I will sow a seed of honesty upon the bluebell knoll

Arise, arise, my clansmen all!
Address a thousand hearers
Those workers of the evil eye
Will tremble and they'll fear us
And all those who would take up the quest
And so turn into heroes
Must walk the narrow path that leads
'Tween Thanatos and Eros

And joy to those who'd use their songs
As clues to lose their clan
But woe to those who'd use them
To enslave their fellow man
Or their fellow woman

Robert Burns wrote a song entitled 'Song Composed in August', first drafted in 1775 when he was sixteen years of age. Some 235 years later this song came along and was given its title in tribute to Burns. Rafe Fitzpatrick wrote and delivered the Welsh 'Rap Y Clychau Glas' that comes before the final chorus in the recorded version; it is reproduced in an appendix to the present volume with thanks to him for taking on the task with righteous passion and good humour.

The End of Breeding

It fell upon a Lammas eve
The spectral pack had come a-souling
No star in all of heaven's weave
Only lonely thunder rolling
I heard the very heavens tell
'Lachrymae et semper dolens'
In roundelay of doleful knells
Dreamed I heard the old bell tolling

Her carnal song unbridles vice
And brings her father to despair
With phantom limbs of fire and ice
Sprawling in the sulphured air
With honey eyes and ruby lips
Silvered in the moon's eclipse
What burning marl of hell is this:
A coffin or a chrysalis?

In her is the end of breeding
In her is the end of breeding
In her is the end of breeding
In me is a brae of weeping
Hers the keys of every treasure
Hers the keys of every treasure

Hers the keys of every treasure
Mine a grieving beyond measure

First I saw the pythoness
And all of her attendant seers
Draw a cypress breath to scream
In Dionysus' ear
Because we two were sib
And shared a greasy drivel-bib
And lay together in one crib
Bony hide to fleshless rib
They send the fell catastrophists
With grasping fists and fiery eyes
To take whichever way they list
Your craven arms and brazen thighs
And then a choir of mendicants
To make calendrical amendments
And raise a voice in endless chant
With all their forebears and descendants

Festival's in misery
Carnival's in lamentation
It's time to take the warring seas
It's time to quit this backlogged nation
And fare thee well, Caledonia!
Fare thee well now and forever
You'll find me in the lowland realm
Of proud Epona and Minerva

And when will you return again?
Tell to me, my new-found brother
'When chords consent to song's intent
Like sire and child and happy mother
And if ever I return again
It's after winter mirk and dreary
'In menso februario hibernum credi expellere'

In me is the end of breeding
In me is the end of breeding
In me is the end of breeding
In her is a brae of weeping
Mine the keys of every treasure
Mine the keys of every treasure
Mine the keys of every treasure
Hers a grieving beyond measure

Wrought under the spell of Rabelais (through the prism of Bakhtin), this is truly a gothic phantasmagoria. 'The Ear of Dionysius' is a cave in Sicily. The sentence in Latin is quoted from an early source by Mircea Eliade in Patterns in Comparative Religion, *but I believe it ought properly to read:* In menso februario hibernum credit expellere. *It is a reference to an early Germanic fertility festival, Spurcalia, believed to have taken place in the month of February.*

The Merry Wake

Will you come to the merry wake, my bonny lassie?
Will you come to the merry wake, my bonny bride?
Come to the merry wake all for your lover's sake
Bonny Saint Kentigern stands upon Clyde

All the day long we'll be drinking like masons
Mixing the gunpowder into the wine
Fixing our liquor in baptismal basins
Bonny Saint Kentigern stands upon Tyne

Choirs of liars are silently keening
The gospel of woman, the mirror and comb
See the deniers, they bring a demeaning
Religion that rose from the sewers of Rome

The sound of our music is shrouded in linen
The pipe and the drum under cold iron sway
Venerable Ossian and noble MacCrimmon
Will lay down their weapons and soon pass away

The whole of the kingdom is clouded in brimstone
Sons against fathers and fathers 'gainst sons
Collar to shoulder and thighbone to shinbone
There never was heard such confusion of tongues

In hour of mayhem, in time of misgiving
Some turn to pastor, some turn to priest
Some would consort with the miserable living
But we'd rather sport with the gleeful deceased

So strike up the cèilidh and lay down your burdens
The Queen of the Unseen Abode's in the room
It's not the round reel, it's not the Gay Gordons
But she'll dance a dark Morris all over your tomb

The Ranter and the Shaker and the wife of the Quaker
Under the cypress tree all join hands
The glum undertaker will take to their maker
Their bodies, relieved of all tiresome demands

The scribes and the clerics like tribes of hysterics
Will hectically dervish and turn widdershins
Be merry until they heretically perish
Then ascend on their merits or swing for their sins

And the Lord lends his everlasting arms
In an answer to your little prayers
For the womb that begets and the worm that devours
So fling yourself into a posture of rapture
A new world will rise from the ruins of ours

Will you come to the merry wake, my bonny lassie?
Will you come to the merry wake, my bonny may?
Come to the merry wake for your lover's sake
New world is only a cockstride away

It is supposed that the sadly persecuted early followers of Christ in Rome would have gathered for clandestine worship in that city's great cloacal spaces. The characterisation of Christianity as 'demeaning' in this song is meant to suggest an abasement of the self before God, rather than implying anything derogatory about the faith or its adherents.

Fusion of Horizons

Love is a fusion of horizons
It stupefies us the more it wisens
The more it wisens, it stupefies us
When we're alive it's all that drives us on
The very end of all our striving
And when we die it will survive us all

Love is a trellis of early roses
A shady arbour the soul encloses
Never jealously imposes
Fellowship on one who'd be alone
It's a holy wand of gnosis
It's a wonder working stone

When we hear that sickbed summons
See the body waste and weaken
When the lowly boneyard beckons
How the curse of grieving deepens then
In the web of unreal feeling
There it seems that love is far and gone

It's a good thing in the morning
It's the reason for our rising
By the evening it's a bad thing
It's the cause of our not thriving
It's a test, a mental harness
It's a lesson sent to learn us well
It's a mess, a mental harness
It's a lesson sent to learn us well

With misery lurking below the surface
How can a man or a woman flourish
But by the gladness that love encourage
Or by the working of some higher purpose?
It will fly, a fiery arrow,
Through the craw of all-devouring time

I can't claim to fully comprehend the hermeneutic concept, drawn from the philosophy of Hans-Georg Gadamer, from which this song's title is pilfered (in an English translation of the original German Horizontverschmelzung*), but I found the turn of phrase a stimulating starting point. The verse form 'Standard Habbie' was customarily used from the eighteenth century onwards, first for elegiac verse and later for comic (e.g. Robert Burns's 'To a Haggis'). Here instead I use a 'Non-standard Habbie' form of my own devising, which seems adept at carrying both elegiac and comic voices simultaneously.*

The Laverock in the Blackthorn

When rain pours down to waken
The laverock in the blackthorn
She sings of all the aching
In our Scotia of the ills

When wind blows in to quicken
The blackbird in the aspen
She sings of how we sicken
Of Breadalbane's rolling hills

It is our sorrow sorest
Woe the falling forest
The north wind brings us no rest
And death is in the skies

I know our love's unbraiding
Like water's dark cascading
I see the polestar fading
On our Scotia of the ills

With my soul enwreathed in hemlock
And mind in thrall to death-knock
I wander as a crook-back
Through arid lands and broad

It's a time of bonds and scourges
Many doleful dirges
While the roaring ocean surges
Round our Scotia of the ills

It is our sorrow sorest
Woe the falling forest
The north wind brings us no rest
And death is in the skies

We'll go where none can tame us
We'll go where none can name us
We'll go where none can blame us
Far from Caledonia

Somebody – a friend of a friend – once asserted that, in my songs, all I do is 'list trees'. Here's a piece which won't stand to refute that assertion. It is indebted to the Irish song 'Sean o'Duibhir a Ghleanna', but with the action, so to speak, relocated to Scotland. Breadalbane is a mountainous region to the north of where I was raised.

Dighty Burn

Willie chose to walk abroad
To walk the path of folly-o
Within his lily hand was clawed
Some other bairnie's dolly-o

Dighty's long and Dighty's deep
Dighty's mirk and dreary-o
In Dighty Water now does sleep
The body of our dearie-o

It's neither by the Sauchiehall
And neither by the Clovenstone
But in ahint the Dighty Wa'
His faither stands and maks his moan

It's neither by the Broomielaw
And neither by the High-Low Stair
But in aneath the Dighty Shaw
His mither sits and reives her hair

And she will pull the bounteous yew
Through the broken ribs of Christ
As fine a tree as ever grew
Beyond the gates of paradise

And of the yew she'll weave a gown
To bind her boy and lie him down
And down will flow her mourning tears
Beyond the standstill of the spheres

This song was commissioned to accompany Dighty, *a short film by Dundee-based artists Edward Summerton and Michael Windle. The lyric became, in part, a pretext to showcase some of my favourite Scottish toponyms. Dighty is the name of a burn in Dundee. The penultimate verse paraphrases a traditional Gaelic charm printed in Alexander Carmichael's* Carmina Gadelica.

Song of the Marvels

Tell me the marvels you saw on your rambles
Tell me the marvels you saw on your rambles
Tell me the marvels you saw on your rambles
Tell me the marvels you saw on your rambles

I saw: A calabash in Amarillo
Flaminica all dressed in yellow
Bluebells in the high Pass of Brenner
And Edelweiss in old Vienna
Tesserae in low Ravenna
And fiddle bows in high Cremona

Tell me the evils you saw on your rambles
Tell me the evils you saw on your rambles
Tell me the evils you saw on your rambles
Tell me the evils you saw on your rambles

I saw: A wave in doldrum, ever drowning
A maid in Bedlam, ever frowning
A lisping sibyl, ever lying
A man imprisoned, ever dying

Tell me the heroes you saw on your rambles
Tell me the heroes you saw on your rambles

Tell me the heroes you saw on your rambles
Tell me the heroes you saw on your rambles

I saw: both Hannibal and bold Alexander
Hannibal and bold Alexander
They sang a new song with all the answers
Aspiring to propaganda

And it went something like this:

One blasphemous mass on the lips of a bishop
Two treacherous tracts on the doors of a church
Three rancorous rants on the lips of a bigot
Four dangerous dances in woodland of birch
Five languorous glances from dancer to dancer
Six cancerous marks on the flanks of a chancer
Seven living laverocks, seven living laverocks
And eight are the questions without any answer
Nine is the shining moon-o
The shining moon is nine-o

A silly piece (in the middle ground between that word's original meaning in Old English and its contemporary resonances) which owes something to 'The Song of Amergin' and 'The Dilly Song'. Some of the geographical references found their way in during a transalpine European tour with Bill Callahan.

Peacock Strut

Then there came travellers, travellers three
Happening randomly by-o
I'll tell you the names of these travellers three:
Listless and Fitful and Sly-o

Fitful to trade was a sharpener of blades
You never saw one so vain-o
A barrel of ash where his heart should have been
And a bramble in place of a brain-o

Listless instead was a blunter of blades
The ugliest witch in this coven
He'd spend all his days devising new ways
To disprove what Fitful had proven

And Sly, who was he? O, he was a man
So fond of me but more fond of a dram
And he was the head of this terrible clan
And 'Touch not the cat' was their slogan

They used the heft of the heron so deft
To outdo me
They used the might of the magpie in flight
To screw me

But such heft and such might, they struck me as slight
With tail in display I scared them away

'Cause I come from a long line of peacocks
I come from a long line of peacocks
Give thanks to the Lord that we can afford
To bear such a burden of feathers

There's no need to tell our endeavours
There's no need to tell our endeavours
No need to tell, no need to tell
No need to tell

Some years ago the great English songwriter Mary Hampton introduced me to the concept of the 'handicap principle'. This is a hypothesis in the field of evolutionary biology which posits that creatures purposely signal their fitness for breeding through extravagant, self-handicapping displays or through dangerous, risky behaviours. The idea is that less fit individuals of the species would be less able to afford such costly strategies. The peacock's huge burden of tail feathers is a particularly visually striking example – perhaps the animal kingdom's equivalent to such human endeavours as smoking, heavy drinking and bungee jumping. 'Touch not the cat bot a glove' is the slogan of Clan Chattan.

Plaint of Lapwing

What cares the crow for the plaint of lapwing?
What cares the snow for the summer's thaw?
Or Orion's bow for the sting of scorpion
Or the heads of Europe as they roll awa'?

Well, I asked the sun, ever westward heading
'Fair Flower Aspect, come cast your craft
Come bring some love to a chymical wedding'
But the answer came as shield to shaft

It's a pox upon you, a pox upon you
Three times a pox on your unholy name
A pox upon you, a pox upon you
And a blessing on all who would you profane
Now knife is in chest, poison in horn
Famine and pest and babies unborn
Knife is in chest, poison in horn
Famine and pest and babies unborn

What cares the wren for the jinx of wryneck
Or the plagal cadence for the dominant chord
Or the dolmen low for the high cathedral
Or the in-sewn hero for the dormant lord?

Well, I asked the moon in her starry carriage
'Come cast your glamour, come cast some more
Come bring some love to a luckless marriage'
And the answer came as wave to shore

It's a blessing on you, a blessing on you
Three times a blessing on your holy name
A blessing on you, a blessing on you
And a pox on any who would you profane
The sun's in the west and all are reborn
All will have rest in the webs of the Norn
The sun's in the west and all are reborn
All will have rest in the webs of the Norn

The meaning of the lapwing, according to Robert Graves, is 'disguise the secret'. 'Fair Flower Aspect' is Blodeuwedd of Welsh mythology. Wrynecks are of the genus Jynx. *'In-sewn' is* Eiraphôitês, *an epithet of Dionysus.*

Anankë

May the horny-handed carpenter
Make me a house and make it good
In the area of house-building
I trust him who knows the ways of wood

May the nimble-fingered shoemaker
Make me some shoes and mak 'em weel
In the area of shoemaking
I trust him who knows toe from heel

May the merry fiddling tailor
Make me a shirt and make it fine
In the area of tailoring
I trust him who knows the warp of twine

Whether I dwell in hall or hovel
Whether I tread in stocking or shoe
Whether I go in rag or robe
One thing, one thing only's true:
He who would alter a thing long ordained
He labours in folly and vanity

Who is the threader of the needle?
And who is the orderer of all our estates?
Who is the holder of the spindle
And who is the architect of all our fates?

Anankë, it's Anankë who built my house
Anankë, it's Anankë who made my shoes
Anankë, it's Anankë who made my shirt
Anankë, it's Anankë by whom we are all begirt

It may seem like the three Fates — the spinner, measurer and cutter — are in charge, but their mother, whose Roman counterpart is Necessitas, is the real boss. Neverthless, the fateful sisters make at least three appearances in the present volume (see, for example, 'Hurricane Brown', p. 110, and 'A Keen', p. 144). The character of the 'fiddling tailor' danced in from another song — the Scottish Gaelic waulking song 'Fosgail an doras dhan tàillear fhìdhleir'. He is also a tailoring fiddler, and, of course, doors — all doors — must be opened for him.

The Wronged Blacksmith

Never wrong a blacksmith
If you would ask him to shoe your pony
Never wrong a blacksmith
If you would have your pony shod
For he'll gather all the scraps
The hammer leaves upon the anvil
Fortune will never travel
The nag will only plod

The animal will only amble
The animal will only amble
The animal will amble
In the mire and the clod

There'll be ruination
Only ruination
Nought but ruination

Never wrong a blacksmith
If you would ask him to arm your army
Never wrong a blacksmith
If you would have your army armed
For he'll temper every arrowhead
And every blade with the antimony

None will face the wrath of them
And come unharmed

None will cross the path of them
None will face the wrath of them
None will cross the path of them
And come home unharmed

Some would say the blacksmith
Already drew his last breath
And he's shackled in the clasp of
Some burning star core
Ah, but he's been at the furnace
And soon he will return with
A darker art to learn us
Than ever before

A darker art to learn us
A darker art to learn us
A darker art to learn us
Than ever before

There'll be ruination
Only ruination
Nought but ruination
Fucking ruination

A song in honour of Goibniu, or perhaps Gofannon, whose name lives on in the sacred township of Govan on the southern shore of the River Clyde. This song features one of only two occurrences in this volume of a particular profanity which I deploy with far greater regularity in my daily speech than in my songs. With apologies to C. Spencer Yeh – not for the profanity, but for appropriating the name of one of his musical projects as a suggested final resting place of the song's antagonist.

If There Is Any Light

It's a country of absence and lack
That the old moon goes hastening through
Curved like a vine-pruner's back
Dimming on poplar and yew

On the rich in their feathery beds
On the poor by their low chimney corners
On the living the same as the dead
And on midwives the same as on mourners

Well, here comes the auld Duke o' Perth
And the folks all give ear to his blethers
He's as haughty as any on earth
Who trod in such fine shoes of leather

And canny as any who yearn
For riches and treasures so gay
But even the nobly born
In the end will descend to the clay

It's a country of bounty and glut
That the new moon goes ambling through
Curved like an emperor's gut
Dimming on me and on you

On the queen in her glittering bower
On the beggar who waits at the entrance
On the lord in his ivory tower
On the wretch on the stool of repentance

Well, here come the men of the road
And the folks run away when they enter
As hardy as any who trod
Round the country full many's the winter

And wily as any who go
In rags and in ribbons so bright
For even the humbly born
In the end will ascend to the light

This was written very quickly in one afternoon when I facilitated a songwriting workshop for younger folks as part of the Edinburgh Youth Gaitherin 2012. The participants were about to embark on a project exploring the sound archives of the School of Scottish Studies as a source for their own creative work. I am put in mind of some words from a traditional song held in that resource – the final verse of William Sharp Lonie's version of the ballad of 'The Laird o' Drum', recorded in Midlothian in 1962: 'When you are deid and I am deid / And both laid in one grave-o / And through the coorse o' time be lifted up again / They'll no' ken your dust fae mine-o'.

Hurricane Brown

Ride the road with me, with me
O Hurricane Brown
So brisk and bold, so frank and free
Ride the road with me
O Hurricane Brown

As borderless as any cloud
O Hurricane Brown
As ever soared the world around
Round and round and round
O Hurricane Brown

Deep in the redwoods one October night
Where the baubles are gaudy and the laughter is bright
It's there that I find her and try to unite
Her body inconstant, her spirit in flight

To be her protector, my never-born daughter
And blissfully wish her the best of all futures
Though the long nimble fingers of the Three Fatal Sisters
Are viciously twisting the future away
Though the weavers are stitching innumerable fictions
In hopes to deceive her and lead her astray

She spins like a pinwheel, she's never known rest
Deep in the deserts of the weather-blown west
It's there that I find her I'm trying to love
I sidle behind her, I hover above

But she needs no protector, my never-born daughter
She's holding before her the best of all futures
And the Three Fatal Sisters can twist all they wish to
The weavers can stitch up their fictions so false
But nothing is stronger than the Parable Speaker
And nothing is weaker than we when he calls

You know I'm a seeker and a friend of the people
To hold all men equal was ever my goal
But sometimes a glimmer of evil comes creeping
I don't know much then but I know I done wrong

I know that I owe you much more than this weakness
Much more than the bleakness of a beast of a man
I owe you forever, the way I betrayed you
Til I may repay you, I give you a song
I owe you forever, the way I betrayed you
Til I may repay you, I give you a song

I went to Montréal for a week with some other Scottish musicians, and this song about an earlier North American adventure was the main thing to emerge.

Honour Song

Well, I'm singing an honour song for a never-born brother
Who gives me the look of one fatherless man to another
Who reckons his pain to be deeper and sweeter than others
I'm singing an honour song with all the love I can muster

Where once was accord and it gladdened the Lord
Now there's only disharmony reigning
He takes a long sup, cup after cup
Of the poison of family draining
Far better indeed for him to be down
On the bosom of company leaning
Remembering a time when it all was so fine
And the world seemed to gleam with new meaning

With all of the wine and the whisky a-flowing
Flowing within him
He was no use to the women who crowded
Lovingly around him

With all of the universe growing so grim and bewildering
He finds a long home in the loam for his body to moulder in
And shudders to hear his obituary babbled by children
Chilled by their laughter, 'Ha-ha!' in its endless unfolding

A song for an old friend who succumbed at a fearfully young age to a terrible disease.

The Mossy Shrine

My heart was waiting on the frontier
On the frontier and all alone
It being a hard, unyielding country
For my pillow I took a stone
As it grew colder upon the frontier
I lay me down by your mossy shrine
Around my shoulders I drew a mantle
Of the wandering stars aligned

Like amulets and talismans
Amulets and talismans
Amulets and talismans
In the palm of every living hand

My heart was waiting on the frontier
On the frontier and all alone
It being a hard, unyielding country
For my pillow I took a stone
And there I dreamed of the pain of childbed
Although the agony was none of mine
When I awakened, the stars had all fled
My stony pillow was broke in twain

And strangler figs and fennel wands
Strangler figs and fennel wands
Strangler figs and fennel wands
Springing from that hard, unyielding land

Written in memory of a flamenco song I heard in Vejer de la Frontera, Andalusia, which featured the conceit of a stone pillow broken in two by the strength of the sleeper's grief.

The Final Diviner

When morning comes and we arise
We rub our eyes and see disaster
On the land and in the skies
Disaster thrives in every place it goes
Still on my face a frown and smile
Are ever striving to be master
As though the thing my brain denies
My soul accepts, and so the struggle shows

I saw a crowd of cunning folk
A-clustered round the inglenook
And when the Final Diviner spoke they all did heed him
Saying, 'Every move the player makes
The puzzle-maker's made before:
In solitaire or tug-of-war there is no freedom'

We'll lay the toys of warfare down
Yet still arise and be victorious
We'll join our hands in friendly bonds
And we will rise and kick the world afore us
We'll lay the toys of warfare down
Break any law that would restrict us
We'll join our hands in friendly bonds
And we will kick the world afore it kicks us

The broader spreads a fellow's frown
The keener wit there is within him
The loud laugh a fellow sounds
The tinier mind there is inside him

I should have looked for such a truth
When standing by the barker's booth
But when the Inner Controller spoke I just ignored him
Saying, 'Every grove you worship in
The Son of Man's already been:
You go within the nemeton, you die of boredom'

Thanks to Rafe Fitzpatrick for the thought-world opened up by 'Gurru'r Byd O'mlaen', and thanks to Eddie Butcher for 'Heather Down the Moor', the tune of which gives this song its lilt.

In Dispraise of Hunger

Now after Lammas there comes a harvest
And after harvest, after harvest
The Lenten fast
And after Nollaig a time of bounty
And after bounty, after bounty
The hungry gap
Till dawns a morning when earthly plenties
Will spread uncounted, spread uncounted
In every lap

Although the table be long unladen
And hunger fading the rosy faces
Of young and old
We thank the ploughman, the weary ploughman
Who turns his hands and his bony fingers
To dig and sow
Till dawns a morning of many graces
Of prayer granted and bread unwanted
In every bowl

We will sing a song in dispraise of hunger
Of the belly and of the soul
Sing a song in dispraise of hunger
Of the belly and of the soul

*In time of lack we'll travel south
And croon it from a leaner mouth
We will sing a song in dispraise of hunger
Of the belly and of the soul*

A simple humanist grace.

This Uneven Thing

I swore to mend your restless edges
To be the man to bear your pain
So was my word, so were my pledges
However bends the weathervane

But now I find that things are changing
You're ailing on some foreign shore
Far beyond my hope of ranging
O, will I ever see you more?

And had I known it before we courted
That love would be this uneven thing
I'd have put my heart in a box of iron
Chained it down with a leaden ring

A sparrow tangled in the wires
They say he's trapped and may never flee
So was my way and my desire
Until the day you came to me

A Scottish back-formation, or conjectured etymology, of the Appalachian song 'Come All You Fair and Tender Ladies'.

Roomful of Relics

The men have withdrawn and left me alone
Left me alone in a roomful of relics
They handed me down no sceptre, no crown
No robe, no clothing angelic

But they gave me the song, so I carry the song
I carry the song that all men inherit
That some men obtain with only disdain
While others ungrudgingly share it

Who dig where they stand and sing all they find
As if in command of a language divine
Or, clouded in mind, they channel the wind
As if in command of nothing

The specific reliquary is somewhere in Madrid but I would no longer be able to find it. Nevertheless, the question is: whether to side with those who dig, or with those who channel the wind?

Child of the Elements

If wisdom or idiocy send you adventuring
Inwardly bound or externally rambling
And insight or ignorance end your dissembling:
Try to be random! Abandon intention!

The eye will give entry to splendours aplenty
Where man is the answer and never the question
The ear grant a passage to wonders unnumbered
Where woman's the centre of endless invention

Pity the eye that sees on the brim of the ocean
Only the form of a crumbling tumbledown kingdom
But happy the ear that hears in the din of creation
Only the song of our oncoming regeneration

May the child of the elements guide us aright
Child of the elements guide us aright
Give us the ear of all hearing, the eye of all sight
Child of the elements! Guide us aright

It's the eye of the eagle, lopsided and bright
Shrill as a filament brimming with infinite light
The ear of the screech owl, the bride of the night
In wild and inelegant widening, widening flight

One of several trillion possible permutations of this Rubik's cube of a song – try switching the lines around – written in 2014 in Hungary, aptly enough, but never released. Perhaps it's the essential inexhaustibility of it which has so far prevented its realisation in recorded form.

Pangs

Friend of mine, come in to dine
And drink with me now times are harder
Bitter nuts and sour wine
Are all we find within the larder

We wait for one, a priestly son
To take the lead and give the order
The loyal breed will thrive indeed
The day our King comes o'er the border

Remember when the earth was glad
As any creature in her keeping
To open up and take the seed
And meekly yield to any reaping

Now grim decision o'er us hangs
To judge of wronghoods two the lesser:
To lie and languish in our pangs
Or rise and meet with our oppressor

May fortune parch and scorch the tongue
By which their very lives were traded
Far outflung when still so young
To live unsung and die unaided

In the Irish epic Táin Bó Cúilagne *('The Cattle Raid of Cooley') there's a mention of 'the men of Ulster lying in their pangs'. Some conjecture that this is a reference to a form of* couvade, *sympathetic labour pains experienced by men, perhaps in a ritualised form.*

The Downward Road

For the downward road is crowded
With underhand and demanding men
For the downward road is crowded
With underhand and demanding men
And how the unblemished one was hounded
As he rode in glory down the glen
For the downward road is crowded
With underhand and demanding men

Sparrows twelve were the birds he moulded
Moulded of the living clay
Sparrows twelve were the birds he moulded
Moulded of the living clay
Breathed a breath and their wings unfolded
Swore and oath and they soared away
Sparrows twelve were the birds he moulded
Moulded of the living clay

A town of scoundrels he turned to sandhills
All on an unforgiving day
A town of scoundrels he turned to sandhills
All on an unforgiving day
A running gangrel he brought to standstill
He will go no further on his way
A town of scoundrels he turned to sandhills
All on an unforgiving day

For the downward road is crowded
With underhand and demanding men
For the downward road is crowded
With underhand and demanding men
And how the unblemished one was hounded
As he rode in glory down the glen
For the downward road is crowded
With underhand and demanding men

This song borrows its title from an African-American spiritual. There is the influence in it of some of the apocryphal accounts about the infancy of Jesus Christ; as such, I tentatively offer it as a possible addition to a canon including far older songs such as 'The Bitter Withy' and 'The Cherry Tree Carol'.

The Angry Laughing God

What god alive would scheme and strive
To keep the peopled earth in check
And deem it meet to wrap his hands
In anger round our narrow necks
Bestow on him a barren sack
Bequeath to her a fallow sex
Gehenna for the many damned
And heaven for the few elect?

Childlessness is no disgrace
But whither now
Whither now the human race?

Long before this old grey beard
Before my curly locks were thinning
Hope was for a welcome woman
Trailing in a gown of linen
Hope was for a bonny brood
All gaily playing in the garden
I their only cornerstone
She their watcher and their warden

I stumbled in disguised in drink
Described an arc around the room
Saw her in the corner shrink
A young embroidress at her loom
Oh, must it be from risk I think
To run like some reluctant groom
And leave her with her maidenhead
In bridal bed as if entombed?

Childlessness is no disgrace
But whither now
Whither now the human race?

Now her apron's to her shin
Her head upon my shoulder resting
Upon her face the wanton grin
Of one with modesty in question
Whatever led her to my door
Is far beyond my understanding
So why should I give roving over
And all my roguery abandon?

It's what the angry laughing god
Who wrought the clockwork universe ordains
To bind with briars our desires
And lock our love away in heavy chains
The angry laughing god who moulded
Everyone both young and old in clay
The angry laughing god who made
Our limbs a loan to be repaid one day

Imagine the bastard offspring of Hobbes and Malthus, brought up on a diet of Calvinist predestinarian doctrine. It isnae bonny.

Wormwood and Gall

Son, you were weaned on the wormwood
Weaned on the wormwood and gall
Formed in the maw of a stormbird
And borne in her claws like a doll
Laid in the garden of order
With Adam who fathered the Fall
Then swaddled in hawthorn and bedded in bramble
You huddled down under the wall

Oh, the wormwood
Oh, the gall

Mother was feared in the wildwood
Revered in her queenly disdain
Entrusted alone with the wise wound
The grime of unbroken campaign
A tongue in her head like a razor
Betrays every shame of my youth
My brazen displays of crazy behaviour
Taken as tokens of truth

Oh, the wormwood
Oh, the gall

Father appeared in my dreaming
The first time I'd seen him in years
Although he was bonny and beaming
My brown eyes were streaming with tears
He took up an old crooked sixpence
To silver the water so blue
And looked to the distance to brood on the fluke
Of existence with unwavering view

Oh, the wormwood
Oh, the gall

I grew up beside a former woollen mill which had been turned into a tourist shop selling scarves and jumpers, tartan things and various Highland trinkets. Although the mill was defunct, the millwheel still turned in the millpond. A sign by the pond declared that all coins thrown therein would be donated to those blinded in war. This song is a crooked sixpence to silver the water for my neighbour, auld Sandy Galloway, one of whose jobs it was to drain the millpond every day to collect the offerings. Apologies to Edward Perronet for pilfering the song's title from a line in the fifth stanza of his hymn 'All Hail the Pow'r of Jesus' Name'.

No Dawn Song

Sing no dawn song, sing no dawn song
You'll waken the baby a-dreaming
Dreaming so long, dreaming so long
Under the eaves in the morning

And in his dream clasp, a casket of glass
The same in the hands of his father
Thereon inscribed: 'There's nothing to hide –
Each holds the key to the other'

Sing no dusk song, sing no dusk song
You'll waken the father a-sleeping
Sleeping so long, sleeping so long
On the green loaning of evening

And in his dream gaze, a balance of days
The same in the eyes of his infant
For time is the way the spendthrift repays
The deepening debts of the skinflint

The songs of my boyhood were callow and candid
Revealing far more than the hearer demanded
Whenever invidious words are rewarded
It's then I'll remember the songs of my boyhood

Measured and guarded, the songs of my wizening
They end as they started, in generous listening
And when I move into my doting and drooling
It's then I'll recover my songs as a young thing
And when I grow into my doting and drooling
It's then I'll re-enter my dreams as a young thing

Looking both backwards and forwards as if at the centre of a mirror; neither an alba *nor an* aubade. *The 'green loaning' crept in from Jean Elliot's 'The Flowers of the Forest'.*

An Altar in the Glade

Well, I startled a deer in the wood
And I saw her run away
She darted down a road
And I chased her all day
A tree gave a creak to my left
And a shudder to my right
As she hurtled down a cleft
And she vanished out of sight

Well, I charted her tracks as I could
To an altar in the glade
Hewn of marble crude
Where often I'd prayed
I cornered her there where she stood
Dappled in the sun
She had a broken leg
And I had a broken gun

Ugly sang the hoodie craw
Some unsuspecting vermin vexing
Hovering low with opening jaw
With undrawn claw and tendon flexing

Fouler still the herring gull
Come to cull the hungry nestling
Hollow old skull and feathers all dull
On whirring pinions never resting

This is the first of two lyrics written while enjoying the hospitality of the Benedictine community of Pluscarden Abbey, Morayshire. A fantasy grounded in ruminations upon some walks in the craggy woods near the abbey.

Vespers Chime

In the dimming of the day
Vespers chime and fade away
Lintie sings all on a spray
To welcome in the evening

Brother on brother streaming through
From barn and byre to row and pew
In hopes of being redeemed anew
Of world and body fusing

Retire as one at dayligone
Rise again to meet the dawn
With canticle and antiphon
All voices interweaving

Though many years have filled their cells
With soldier's dice, with pilgrim shells
They've emptied out their sorry selves
The better to receive us

And live in magnificence if they can
Magnificence

After hours of solemn thanks
Comes a time for monkish pranks
Retreat awhile and so advance
Among the unbelieving

All who would the Name profane
In bearing loss, in craving gain
Within the walls they may remain
Or leave of their own choosing

As ever yet, the day must close
Each, unalike, will find repose
To dream on where the lintie goes
Along the skyway cruising

Though many years have swelled our souls
With older vice than we can know
We've emptied out our sorry selves
The better to receive you

And live in magnificence if we can
Magnificence!

The second of the two lyrics from Pluscarden, this one on the theme of kenosis. Thanks to the great Michael Longley for 'dayligone', an Ulster word which hopefully sounds truly enough on the tongue of a Scotsman.

Scarce of Fishing

The heaving ocean, so scarce of fishing
Unfinished mission, forsaken hearth
So many striving against all wishing
To force a living from the broken earth

The harbour women their breasts are bearing
Each woman wearing her mother's skin
For lovers leaving on the tide a-seething
And each one grieving abandoned kin

I hear one call upon a breeze unceasing
To coax an ember to leaping flame
Below the fallen beams of the home we're leaving
And open up an untold store of pain

For all the many forced by fell circumstance to leave their homes (wheresoever they may be) and loved ones (whomsoever they may be) in the hope of a better existence overseas. The title is a translation of the Gaelic 'Spìocaireachd Iasgaich', which is also the name of a piobaireachd *composition.*

False Flesh

It was all around the time of the final Embertide
When the may was all a-bloom and bloom a-drifting
Down the long and bony road by the narrow riverside
There a hollow bride I spied and she was stumbling
Stumbling down the bony road with a tremor in her head
And from pleasure into dread forever shifting
Well, she took me unaware, she disturbed the very air
With the fervour of her prayer, hard and humbling:

Fall away, false flesh
Fall away, oh!
Fall away false flesh
Fall away, oh!

I will roam around the breadth
Of the many-splendoured earth
'Mid the men of phony flesh, although they spurn me
Though they'd send me to my death
From my dwelling in the breast
Of the one supernal spouse they'll never turn me
I'll condemn them in a verse
I'll offend with every breath
Just an anchoress intoning her confession

Those who act as if they've earned
Their reward in the beyond
Ere the reckoning day has dawned will learn their lesson

Oh, shifty old God, the first of your gifts,
The joy of our youth, you soon remove
Oh, shifty old God, the last of your gifts,
The fastness of death, we'd fain refuse

Fall away, false flesh
Fall away, oh!
Fall away false flesh
Fall away, oh!

This song was written after reading the book of Margery Kempe of mediaeval King's Lynn, recognised as the author of the earliest known biographical writing by a woman in the English language.

A Keen

He trilled like a bird on his day of arrival
I lulled him asleep as he lay in the cradle
He garbled the creed as he stood in the schoolroom
I chanted the lay he would bear as an heirloom
I gave him an heirloom – what more could I do?

Clotho, she sits with her hands on the spindle
Working the silk that the spider delivers
Lachesis allots with industrious fingers
What Atropos cuts with her rusty old scissors

I whispered a grace at the head of the table
He crooned an aubade at the door of his lover
I lilted a reel on their day of betrothal
They billed and they cooed all the summer together
They billed and they cooed all the long summer through

I made a work-song all the days of his raising
He roared out an oath on our final leave-taking
But oh, for the notions of Fate so mercurial
To be wailing a keen on the day of his burial
To be wailing a keen on his burial day

This was written with clarity of purpose in one morning in February 2018, before travelling from Oxfordshire to Glasgow under the watchful eye of 'the beast from the east'. The song grew from an interest in the various usages of music or utterance to mark certain transitional moments in the lives of societies or of individuals.

Europe

Europe was broad, Lord, and Europe was wide
And Europe had need of a groom and a guide
One to unite her long-suffering tribes
A broker of vices, a taker of bribes

Brink of extinction was looming in sight
I took up the rest of my treasures and fled
Before we came into the City of Light
There by the road we discarded our dead

A lover betrayed me, they seized me in bed
They numbered my name and they shadowed my tread
They measured my head for to fathom my soul
Declared me untainted and freed me once more

Although I am only an ordinary man
A detail, a footnote, a snag in the plan
A 'cello, a dresser, a mirror, a room
The struggle has made a phenomenal man

The snows of the fatherland stubborn and cold
The day when the last of my treasures was sold
The sorrows of Zion inscribed on my brow
I think of these things as I sing to you now

I sing of the pawn and the king and the queen
The bishop, the rook and the cuddy
The sidelong retreat and the crabwise advance
The deadlock unending and bloody

I sing of the joker, the ace and the jack
All the rest of the pack in their power
The fine interlinking of risk and of luck
That leads to the fall of a ruler

I watched a documentary on the life of Freddie Knoller BEM, a Holocaust survivor, and was moved to write this song. Born into a Jewish family in Austria in 1921, Freddie defied the Nazis at every turn and escaped with his life, eventually to die at the age of 100 in 2022. 'Cuddy' is a Scots word for a horse or donkey; it was the word my late father used (and which, as a result, I continue to use) for the chess piece usually known in English as the knight.

The Evernew Tongue

In January as it befell
I lay dumbfounded in my weatherbound cell
Outside in the drifting snow
Revellers come and revellers go
Here upon our Hogmanay
Sing the old year bleary-eyed away
All among our huddled kin
Sing the new year muddle-headed in
Good be to our humble home
From roofbeam high to low hearthstone!

Every song that's never more sung
Will sound again upon the Evernew Tongue

Although we hear the cries and jeers
The mocking whine of demagogues
In whose minds all falsehoods grind
Creaking gears and interlocking cogs
We curse those lips so quick to mock
Quick to mock and yet so slow to bless
Also those hard unloving eyes
Eyes which only prize all worldly wealth
Open up their broken home
And welcome in the Man of Bone

Every wrong that's ever been done
Will find its end in the Inscrutable One
Ever song that's never more sung
Will sound again upon the Evernew Tongue

A Hogmanay song, partly inspired by a traditional Orcadian New Year rhyme: 'Guid be tae this buirdly biggin' / Fae the steethe-stane tae the riggin'!'. In Tenga Bithnúa *('The Evernew Tongue') is a mediaeval Irish text, composed in the ninth or tenth century and purporting to reveal the mysteries of the creation, of the cosmos, and of the end of the world as related by the soul of the Apostle Philip speaking in the language of the angels. I offer great thanks to David Tibet for providing me with a copy of that text.*

Actors

Our masters distract us with catches and glees
Unnatural laughter and vacuous rage
Ah, but we will unmask them, unmask them with ease
For we are the actors, we've taken the stage

Our patrons are wallowing in great velvet seats
So keenly suspending their deep disbelief
As long as they're following our ploys and deceits
Our fate runs to glory and never to grief

As long as we're comic, the crowd is in tears
But when we wax tragic they sit there tight-lipped
We give them wild magic, they block up their ears
Yet they turn a blind eye when we stick to the script

And when we've departed the critics will rave
'The casting was matchless, the staging was brave
It fractured in places but still we must praise
The fact that those actors commanded our gaze'

Not many words can have entered modern English from the relatively mysterious language of the Etruscans, spoken in northern Italy before the expansion of Rome, but one such word is 'person'. It's thought to derive from phersu, *denoting the mask worn by a theatrical actor.*

The Stranger with the Scythe

Or would you trifle your life away
With every eyeful of strife you face
Or crave oblivion the livelong day
Your body shrivelling without a trace

When all you swear by, sham or fact –
Gloomy musings in an almanac
Or whimsy scribbled in the shifting sand –
Will meet the editor's ever-redacting hand?

The vulture circles above the kirk
He knows our dirty sepulchral work
He'll be the one to whom we vainly pray
To keep the stranger with the scythe at bay

And see the woman with the rheumy eyes
You'd never envy her unhappy prize
To be a widow long before a wife
All to the stranger with the shining scythe

And see the skinny fiddler twist and writhe
You never heard a music more alive
And in the end a slippery jig she plays:
'A Quiet Passage to a Welcome Grave'

Or would you trifle your life away
With every eyeful of strife you face
Or crave oblivion the livelong day
Your liver shrivelling without a trace?

A piece of grotesquerie, the musical arrangement of which features some fruity chromaticism influenced by a barbershop singing workshop I'd recently attended. The workshop was led by Rory Haye, who subsequently wrote the vocal harmony which features in the studio version of the song. The skinny fiddler's jig is by Izaak Walton.

Learning Is Eternal

All about the slack end of the year
When the winter sun's declining
There comes on earth a birth of births
All other births outshining
All other births outshining

And then at last a death of deaths
All other deaths undoing
'Tween birth and death there spans a life
All others redefining
All others redefining

And when I traced Our Lady's face
In the lily-flower a-budding
In stem and seed, in word and deed
Her ageless blood was flooding
Her ageless blood was flooding

And when I marked our Maker's hand
In the whorl upon the kernel
It's then I came to understand
That learning is eternal
Learning is eternal

Yesterday my bed was grey and I lay alone
I lost my face in hollow clay upon a frame of bone
Tomorrow let my bed be set in a finer room
My form I'll find in marble shining through the gloom

Oh, lucky, lucky youth with room to spread
And the means to range unguarded
No call to rue a squandered breath
Or any boon discarded

May you turn away from funeral games
Turn from dying into living
And spurn all vain and baseless claims
To tenancy of heaven

Every living age has cause to mourn
And blame its ill begetters
Great shame if all the born unbound
Should have to die in fetters

This song emerged, in part, from some ruminations engendered by the wise words of Christopher Mack, 'Learning's Unending', which I paraphrased.

The Tender Hour

Forgive a lovelorn one this ardent suit
Not willing yet to draw a final shroud
O'er something under-formed and undefined
Nor more to stall and let this tongue lie mute
That would proclaim your beauty, honoured friend

Oh, must we pause and wonder what might bloom
And flourish soul by soul and mind to mind
A spark within your eyes of cloudy blue
Igniting now in mine of sable brown
Yet carry such a wondering to our doom?

For hearts that sing as one are rare and few
As frail and simple as a winter flower
Slowly closing under frozen dew
Before awakening in the tender hour
To Love and Love alone, our final end

This started life as an attempted sonnet until it found its tune and took its current shape.

Hymn of Welcome

Laden with a jaded soul
This aged fool for whom the tomb is nearing
Offers up a welcome hymn
To trembling foal from womb door meekly peering

Though I ail, o, child I ail, o
Diminished one from whom the time is fleeing
Though I ail, o, child I ail, o
Unblemished lamb, I sing you into being

Springing from a sinner's throat
A sombre yet a joyful note of greeting
He lays aside all sin to dote
On sapling heart with fresh blood weakly beating

Though I ail, o, child I ail, o
Diminished one from whom the time is fleeing
Though I ail, o, child I ail, o
Unblemished lamb, I sing you into being

He takes a wasted candle-end
The flame that lately raged now pale and dwindled
And bears it with a palsied hand
To light some tiny wick that's ne'er been kindled

He draws around a final shroud
To shield the wind and keep the candle burning
And offers up a humble verse
To guard against the family curse returning

Laden with a jaded soul
Blameless babe, I've known my toll of sinning
But shame will fade and failings wane
To know that in my end is your beginning

The passing on of a flame from one at life's closing to one at its beginning, written some time before I realistically imagined fatherhood as a path upon which I would eventually embark. The voice in the song is not necessarily that of a father to his own child, but perhaps of a generation aware of its failings, regretting and so vainly attempting to ward off the sense of those failings constituting the next generation's inheritance. Admitting the inspiration of Cavafy's poem 'Candles'.

The Green Chapel

By the green chapel, the chapel of ease
I saw the wind whip all the leaves from the trees
I saw the trees bend and I saw the roots buckle
The very earth groaned and the wind seemed to cackle
Where two fond lovers fell down on their knees
By the green chapel of ease

In the green chapel, the chapel of rest
I saw the sun dapple the glass in the west
There all the day with my eyes on the window
I saw the sun rise and I saw the sun dwindle
In the green chapel where love is confessed
In the green chapel of rest

Deep in the chapel, the heart of the chapel
There stands a narrow bed
Its sheets they are silken and white as the milk
Under crimson coverlet spread
Beyond the green chapel I heard of a river
Flowing in the wood
The old fabled river, the half it runs water
The other runs blood

And as it fell out on the eve of the Sabbath
A lullaby rang round the bed
The river ran over with song of great gladness
Lamenting arose in the wood
These three noble strains came and braided together
Entwined in the sign of the Rood
These three noble strains came and braided together
And all was good

The green chapel here is not that of Arthurian legend, but Rosslyn Chapel near Edinburgh, which I visited in good company shortly before this song's conception in early 2019. There are 'three noble strains' of music – goltraí, geantraí *and* suantraí *(respectively, the strains of sorrow, joy and sleep). This song envisions a scenario where these three strains resolve in unbreakable unity. The influence of 'Corpus Christi Carol' is felt.*

Orison of Union

O, the burning sand and the rolling wave
The rocking cradle and the open grave
The fire that rises and the rain that falls
May our love, o, may our love, o
May our fleeting love outlast them all

O, the lofty poplar and the towering pine
The sprawling hawthorn and the tangling vine
As the thriving ivy spites the winter chill
May our love, o, may our love, o
May our feeble love grow stronger still

As the wheeling shadows of the solstice eve
Fill the young with gladness while their elders grieve
The falling, rising of the cutty wren
May our love, o, may our love, o
May our dying love be born again

So meek a bird and yet so grand
Upon our chimney corner land
While I bestow upon your hand
The solemn band of union

And may that bird of omen good
Carol through the gloaming wood
And gladly gift the drifting dawn
An orison of union

A love song (and another list of trees).

The Undiscovered Land

Flowers growing on the mountain
Where the tall trees stand
Easy joys beyond all counting
Over in the undiscovered land

Ferns uncurling in the valley
Where the tall trees stand
Fond ones come to woo and dally
Over in the undiscovered land

Lover, I will come to see you
Will you take my father's hand?
Lover, I will come to see you
In the undiscovered land

Farmers ramble on the mountain
Where the tall trees stand
High above the hawk is haunting
Over in the undiscovered land

Lambkins gambol in the valley
Where the tall trees stand
Feathered songsters warble brawly
Over in the undiscovered land

Father, I will come to see you
Will you take my lover's hand?
Father, I will come to see you
In the undiscovered land

I'll meet you by and by, I'll meet you by and by
On the day we join that happy band
I'll meet you by and by, I'll meet you by and by
Over in the undiscovered land

This was written in London in February 2020; the first lines came during an evening walk along Bethnal Green Road as it buzzed with a hectic pre-pandemic energy. The title is influenced by the similar yet not identical title of a book mentioned to me by a friend a few days beforehand, which is in turn taken from Shakespeare's Hamlet. *I was imagining a meeting impossible on this plane – that between my father and my partner.*

Lorica

Curly-browed and tousle-headed
Shining eyes all bonny beaded
Tiny seed our love has tended
May you be from all harm defended

Catkin fingers newly budded
Couthy mouth and cheeks all ruddy
Like a pearl our love has yielded
May you be from all evil shielded

Grasping arms and legs in spasm
Pistons marking nimble rhythm
Laughing babe our love has granted
May you be by all wrongs undaunted

Primeval dangers are lately mutating
All under the sun, under the moon
And endlessly ranging in
Stronger and stronger strains
Under the sun, under the moon
So summon a prayer against
The world and her share of pains
Under the sun, under the moon
Pray on and pray again

'Til only the prayer remains
Under the sun, under the moon
Love be the name of you
Love in the soul of you
Under the sun, under the moon
Love be the flame in you
The flame be the whole of you
Under the sun, under the moon

Lorica *is a Latin word for 'breastplate', and by extension a protective spell or blessing, as in the well-known mediaeval Irish work 'Saint Patrick's Breastplate'. That is the sense in which the term is used in the title for this song, which was written in anticipation of the birth of my son.*

The Auld Butcher's Apron

When first I awakened, the days they were straitened
The world was befouled and her people were aching
My ways they were shaped in a playpen of mayhem
I brooded and scowled while my playmates were capering
Under the gaze of a murderous matron
Her favour the aim of their bowing and scraping

Now I awaken to find myself facing
A looking-glass world of another man's making
That self-proclaimed statesman disgracing the nation
With every false word and each vain declaration
I cast a last glance of disdain o'er the wasteland
And patiently wait for the one who'll replace him

Those who go draped in the auld butcher's apron
Under the sun, under the moon
Surely the fate of a traitor awaits them
Under the sun, under the moon

Any fellow child of the eighties could make a good guess as to the identity of the 'murderous matron'. As for the identity of the statesman mentioned in the second verse – well, take your pick!

Remembrancer's Blues

Who'll mourn the warmonger when the warmonger dies?
Who'll mourn the warmonger when the warmonger dies?
Who'll mourn the warmonger even his children despise?

I, the remembrancer, crooning over his bones
I, the remembrancer, crooning over his bones
I'll mourn the warmonger even his mother disowns

I mourn the warmonger and I bury the fate
I mourn the warmonger and I bury the fate
Of his long-squandered store and his divided estate

I heard the warmonger claim that the rod of command
I heard the warmonger claim that the rod of command
Fell so heavily into his unready hand

I, the remembrancer, say that this song was unplanned
I, the remembrancer, say that this song was unplanned
But it resounded unbidden when gold crossed my hand

Give him the mantle of black and the glad widow's weed
And the Devil go with him who revels in greed
O, the remembrancer's blues, the remembrancer's blues
The remembrancer's blues are the warmonger's too

Written shortly after the death of a prominent political figure of international notoriety. Probably the only twelve-bar blues I'll ever write.

Appendix 1

The Ruby in the Hawthorn

The following text was written in 2007, part of the same burst of creative activity which gave rise to the Spoils *LP and* The Wyrd Meme *EP. Although 'The Ruby in the Hawthorn' wasn't recorded at that time (and still hasn't been), it was performed in various contexts shortly thereafter. It eventually became part of the fabric of another piece, an 'anti-opera' entitled* Who Will Go Mad With Me? *devised along with Luke Fowler, Sylvia Hallett and David Toop, which premiered at the Huddersfield Festival of Contemporary Music in 2013. Neither that collaborative piece nor the original text have been performed or aired since, and perhaps never will be again.*

'The Ruby in the Hawthorn' is an alchemical cantefable *and might earn the classification of Aarne–Thompson type 592 ('Dancing in Thorns'). 'The Stars Down to Earth' is German philosopher Theodor Adorno's critique of astrology. In Jungian psychology, the ruby signifies the* rubedo *phase of individuation. The character of the fiddling tailor may be familiar from the song 'Anankë', which is reproduced elsewhere in this volume. He is here identified with Jack Orion, the magical fiddler of ballad tradition (cf. 'Glasgerion' [Child 67]). According to Robert Graves in* The White Goddess, *the hawthorn 'is an unlucky tree and the name under which it appears in the Irish Brehon Laws,* sceith, *is apparently connected with the Indo-Germanic root* sceath *or* scēth, *meaning harm, from which derive the English 'scathe' and the Greek* a-scethes, *scatheless.'*

There was a time I don't remember, when I still walked among my people (or perhaps when still between my folks I strolled). I slipped into my old, old road clothes, took off across the Argyll Wold – but it might have been the Celtic Fringe (like I say, my memory's hazy, and on the deep and simple meaning of this very tale I'm telling such distinctions do not hinge).

I came into the deep, deep forest and there I saw a moonlit henge, adorning it the densest hawthorn, the densest one I'd ever seen – the densest one for worlds around, for worlds and worlds and worlds around.

Something glistened in the hawthorn; something shimmered in the hawthorn; something glimmered in the hawthorn – I saw a red, red ruby.

Then I wriggled in the hawthorn; then I squiggled in the hawthorn; at length I struggled with the hawthorn, for it had stuck me truly.

I swore an oath up to Adorno; I swore an oath up to Adorno; I swore an oath up to Adorno:

'Adorno! Bring the stars down!
Adorno! Bring the stars down!
Adorno! Bring the stars down!
Adorno! Bring the stars down!'

> 'I dare no more bring the stars down
> Than Orion bring Edarnon
> Triskelion and Molendinar

> I will shine brighter and finer
> I'll be the only star in this play
> I'll be the only strolling player
> Upon this sloping stage made of air
> You patrons of the lively arts,
> Come line my bowl with your silver!'

By there came a fiddling tailor; by there came a tailoring fiddler; by there came a fiddling tailor, down among the hawthorn.

Well, whoever heard of a fiddling tailor? Whoever heard of a tailoring fiddler? Whoever heard of a fiddling tailor, down among some hawthorn?

He struck a note upon his fiddle and as he played he swirled around. He swirled and swirled and swirled and swirled around, and as he played I came unstuck.

'I could've sworn you were Adorno!
I could've sworn you were Adorno!
I could've sworn you were Adorno
Come to bring the stars down!'

> 'Oh no, oh no, I'm no Adorno!
> Oh no, oh no, I'm no Adorno!
> Oh no, oh no, I'm no Adorno!
> I am Jack Orion!'

'You could've scathed me but you saved me
You could've fiddled me further in
You could've scathed me but you saved me
Barely even trying'

        'That was my father's mistake –
        I have my own to make
        That was my father's mistake –
        Mine is another
        That was our fathers' mistake –
        We have our own to make
        That was our fathers' mistake –
        Ours is another'

He sewed for me some new, new road clothes, took off into the woods alone and left me with the ruby in my hand.

I'm going to build a house, a home, with no windows, with no doors. I'm going to lay this precious stone – bury my ruby – under the threshold.

Appendix 2

Adeus à mágoa (Christopher Mack)

I'm listening to 'Farewell Sorrow' being performed live in a garden shed. Feeling again the impassioned spirit of the song, and certain that it was something of this spirit that urged me to translate it into Brazilian Portuguese.

Translation, at times, affords an opportunity to travel and pass through layers of meaning and to play. As the process is so often tied to a deadline, it is refreshing to work on something for entirely personal ends and unhurriedly re-present meaning.

What made this translation so different was that I would be singing it, and it soon became clear that in wishing to remain true to the vocal melody, the words would have to be sung out loud to see how they might find their place. A new and incredibly enjoyable experience:

Levante-me alto, levante-me alto
Para que possa ver os meus parentes caídos sentados
Que encontraram a morte no campo de guerra
Que, no final, caíram e foram derrotados

E o jeito que foram enganados pela morte
Traídos, traídos, arrasados e maltratados
Já enfiei uma faca num homem por menos
Mas a Morte não é tão facilmente derrotada

E pode rezar, rezar, rezar pela vida
Mas saiba, meu amigo, meu querido amigo, saiba disso
Que a Vida é só o braço direito da Morte
Em cada parte do seu ofício canhoto

Então, de braços dados, correremos até aquele par
E nòs como eles, juntamos em fio duplo
E, de braços abertos, corremos até aquele par
E sem sentir o medo daquilo que uma vez tememos

Christopher Mack

Appendix 3

Rafe's Rap

'Song Composed in December' (incorporating 'Rap Y Clychau Glas') was recorded at the end of April 2012. 'Y Rap' materialised while on Bute one weekend at the end of March or start of April. Walking in woods above Rothesay I finally pulled all the segments together. The reference to Bute came from the connection it has to the Welsh language in the exploitation of the South Wales coalfield and peoples by the Marquess of Bute, hence the line 'Ni'n dod i cymryd Bute' – 'We're coming to take Bute.'

Other references are to pwnco – a poetry contest associated with the New Year tradition Y Mari Lwyd between those in the Mari Lwyd party and those in the houses they visit. Twmpath means a barn dance. 'A oes heddwch?' ('Is there peace?') references the call at Yr Eisteddfod Genedlaethol (The National Eisteddfod) when a bard is crowned or chaired.

I don't know when Ali first had the idea for 'Y Rap', as we played 'Song Composed in December' many times without it. First performing it was very nerve-wracking, but after a few shows I got into the flow and I hope on occasion I channelled some Dave Datblygu in my performance.

What follows is my original rap in Welsh, followed by Alasdair's own translation of it into Scots, and a further translation into Scottish Gaelic by Alasdair and Màiri Morrison.

Rafe Fitzpatrick

Rap Y Clychau Glas

Dewch ynghyd ffrindiau a gwrandewch ar y sŵn
Y Pencerdd Ali R yn pwnco gyda ni
Gwrandewch i'r straeon newydd a clywch am beth mae'n sôn,
Yr hen a'r newydd, gwreiddiau yn yr un
Cymdogion, dewch i'r twmpath a dansiwch trwy's nôs
I'r mwsic heb cymhair sy'n tynnu ni'n glôs
Y clychau glas sy'n seinio, dros yr holl fyd,
Yn galw ni yma i troi o'r ffordd cul
Boncers, bankers y brwydr hyll,
Sy'n cymrud bywyd ddyn a rhacso fe i bits
Cofiwch, sigloch eich meddwl,
A'ch boclyn, ni'n dod i cymryd Bute.

Dŵad yw'r noson dda lloerig.
Heno fydd y cymylau yn cwympo,
Y sêr yn toddi, a'r meddwl yn teithio
Dros filoedd o flynyddoedd i weld
Y dechrau a'r diwedd.
Heno fydd ein seindorf yn canu,
A oes heddwch, a oes heddwch?
Ble mae'r heddwch?

Rafe Fitzpatrick

Rap o' the Blaewort

Draw thegither, freens, an hearken tae the soun:
Heid Makar Ali R flyting wi us!
Listen tae the new tellins an whit they hae tae say,
The auld an the new wi likesome roots.
Neebors! Come tae the cèilidh an dance a nicht
Tae the musick sans peir thit draws us ticht.
The blaewort's ringin athort the warl
Ca'in us here tae turn fae the narra way
Bletherers, thesaurers, the laithly war
That taks a man's life an reives her tae bits.
Tak tent: shak yer mind as weel's yer buckle
We're comin tae tak Bute!

Comin is the guid starry nicht.
This ae nicht the heivins will fa,
The staurn melt, an the mind traivel
Athort thoosans o years tae see
The beginnin an the end.
This nicht oor band will sing
'Is there peace? Is there peace?
Whaur is the peace?'

Translation by Alasdair Roberts

Rap Bròg na Cuthaige

Thigibh còmhla, a chàirdean, agus èistibh ris an fhuaim:
An t-Àrd-Bhàrd Ali R ag argamaid rinn!
Èistibh ris na sgeulachdan ùra agus na tha aca ri ràdh,
Sean agus ùr leis na h-aon freumhan.
Nàbaidhean! Thigibh chun a' chèilidh
Is dannsaibh fad na h-oidhche
Ri ceòl gun choimeas a tharraingeas dlùth sinn.
Bròg na cuthaige a' seirm air feadh an t-saoghail
Gar gairm an-seo gus tionndadh bhon t-slighe chumhang
Bancairean, boncairean, an cogadh grànda
A chuireas às do dhuine agus a bhriseas ann am pìosan ì.
Thoiribh an aire: crathaibh ur n' inntinn a thuilleadh air ur bucaill
Tha sinn a' tighinn gus buaidh a thoirt air Eilean Bhòid!

Tha an oidhche mhath, rionnagach a' tighinn.
Air an oidhche sin fhèin tuitidh na nèamhan
Leaghaidh na reultan agus siùbhlaidh an inntinn
Tro mhìltean de bhliadhnaichean
Gus an toiseach agus an deireadh fhaicinn.
A-nochd seinnidh ar còmhlan:
'Am bheil sìth ann? Am bheil sìth ann?
Càit a bheil an t-sìth?'

Translation by Alasdair Roberts and Màiri Morrison

It's not as a rapper that Rafe first came to my acquaintance, but as a fiddler. We had been enjoying playing music and spending time together for a couple of years; Rafe, a Ceredigion man exiled in Glasgow – happily enough, but nevertheless still in thrall to hiraeth *– played fiddle on the LP* A Wonder Working Stone. *It was in the spirit of international solidarity and in support of suppressed languages that I invited him to write the Welsh language piece which became 'Rap Y Clychau Glas', and it's the same spirit in which I now humbly offer two new translations of it, into Scots and Scottish Gaelic. The latter piece was a co-translation with my Leòdhasach friend, native Gàidhlig speaker Màiri Morrison, whose generous and patient work improved my initial solitary attempt immeasurably.*

Alasdair

Discography

'Autumn' and 'Seagulls, Belts' first appeared on the LP *The Rye Bears a Poison* by Appendix Out (Drag City, 1997).

'Ice Age' first appeared on the 7″ single *Ice Age* by Appendix Out (Palace Records, 1996).

'Exile', 'Tangled Hair' and 'The Grey Havens' first appeared on the LP *Daylight Saving* by Appendix Out (Drag City, 1999).

'Well Lit Tonight (First Perthshire House Song)' first appeared in a recording by Appendix Out on a split 7″ single with the Leopards (Creeping Bent, 1997).

'Second Perthshire House Song' first appeared in a recording by Appendix Out on a split 7″ single with Songs: Ohia (Liquefaction/Bad Jazz, 1998).

'A Cataract in the Cavalry' first appeared under the title 'Ein Grauerstar in der Kavallerie' on the 7″ *Lieder für Kaspar Hauser* by Appendix Out (Western Vinyl, 2000).

'Cyclone's Vernal Retreat' and 'Hexen in the Anticyclone' first appeared on the LP *The Night is Advancing* by Appendix Out (Drag City, 2001).

'The Last House' first appeared on the eponymous EP by Amalgamated Sons of Rest (Galaxia, 2002).

'The Language in Things' first appeared in a recording by Appendix Out on the compilation CD *You Don't Need Darkness to Do What You Think Is Right* (Geographic, 2001).

'I Went Hunting', 'Farewell Sorrow', 'The Whole House Is Singing', 'Come, My Darling Polly', 'I Fell in Love' and 'Slowly Growing Old' first appeared on the LP *Farewell Sorrow* by Alasdair Roberts (Drag City, 2003).

'Hyperboreans' first appeared on the 7″ single *A Selection of Marches, Quicksteps, Laments, Strathspeys, Reels and Country Dances* by Alasdair Roberts and Jackie Oates (Room40, 2010).

'Riddle Me This', 'Waxwing', 'River Rhine', 'The Old Men of the Shells', 'Where Twines the Path', 'Firewater' and 'The Calfless Cow' first appeared on the LP *The Amber Gatherers* by Alasdair Roberts (Drag City, 2007).

'Coral and Tar' and 'The Yarn Unraveller' first appeared on the EP *The Wyrd Meme* by Alasdair Roberts (Drag City, 2009).

'Unyoked Oxen Turn', 'Hazel Forks', 'The Flyting of Grief and Joy

(Eternal Return)', 'So Bored Was I (Dark Triad)', 'Ned Ludd's Rant (For a World Rebarbarised)' and 'Under No Enchantment (But My Own)' first appeared on the LP *Spoils* by Alasdair Roberts (Drag City, 2009).

'The Hidden Sin' first appeared on the soundtrack of the film *All Divided Selves* (dir. Luke Fowler, 2011).

'The Sacred Nine and the Primal Horde' first appeared on the LP *Revenge of the Folksingers by Concerto Caledonia* (Delphian, 2011).

'Haruspex of Paradox' first appeared on the compilation CD *Weirdlore* (Folk Police Recordings, 2012).

'Song Composed in December', 'The End of Breeding', 'The Merry Wake', 'Fusion of Horizons' and 'The Laverock in the Blackthorn' first appeared on the LP *A Wonder Working Stone* by Alasdair Roberts & Friends (Drag City, 2013).

'Dighty Burn' first appeared on the short film *Dighty* (dir. Edward Summerton, Michael Windle) and accompanying 7″ single *Dighty Burn* by Alasdair Roberts (DogTown, 2011).

'The Evening Is Growing Dim', 'Peacock Strut', 'Plaint of Lapwing', 'Anankë', 'The Wronged Blacksmith' and 'If There Is Any Light' first appeared on the LP *Plaint of Lapwing* by Alasdair Roberts and James Green (Clay Pipe, 2016).

'Hurricane Brown', 'Honour Song', 'The Mossy Shrine', 'The Final Diviner', 'In Dispraise of Hunger', 'This Uneven Thing' and 'Roomful of Relics' first appeared on the LP *Alasdair Roberts* by Alasdair Roberts (2015).

'Child of the Elements' is yet to be released.

'Song of the Marvels', 'Pangs', 'The Downward Road', 'The Angry Laughing God', 'Wormwood and Gall', 'No Dawn Song', 'An Altar in the Glade', 'Vespers Chime' and 'Scarce of Fishing' first appeared on the LP *Pangs* by Alasdair Roberts (2017).

'The Untrue Womb', 'False Flesh', 'A Keen', 'Europe', 'The Evernew Tongue', 'Actors', 'The Stranger with the Scythe' and 'Learning is Eternal' first appeared on the LP *The Fiery Margin* by Alasdair Roberts (Drag City, 2019).

'The Tender Hour', 'Hymn of Welcome', 'The Green Chapel' and 'Orison of Union' first appeared on the LP *The Old Fabled River* by Alasdair Roberts og Völvur (Drag City, 2021).

'The Undiscovered Land', 'Lorica', 'The Auld Butcher's Apron' and 'Remembrancer's Blues' first appeared on the download-only EP *Saining Songs* by Alasdair Roberts (Hudson, 2022).

Index of Titles and First Lines

A stranger rapped his staff upon my window   14
Actors   150
All about the slack end of the year   154
An Altar in the Glade   136
Anankë   103
The Angry Laughing God   129
As I roved out one Shrovetide eve   45
The Auld Butcher's Apron   168
Autumn   3
Because my face betrayed a smile   59
By the green chapel, the chapel of ease   160
The Calfless Cow   51
A Cataract in the Cavalry   15
Child of the Elements   122
Cities rarely disappear   15
Come, My Darling Polly   30
Coral and Tar   54
Curly-browed and tousle-headed   166
Cyclone's Vernal Retreat   17
Dighty Burn   95
The Downward Road   126
The End of Breeding   85
Enthralled was I, so enthralled was I   67
Europe   146
Europe was broad, Lord, and Europe was wide   146
The Evening Is Growing Dim   35
The Evernew Tongue   148
Exile   9
False Flesh   142
Farewell Sorrow   26
The Final Diviner   116
Firewater   49
First thing she gave me: 71
Flowers growing on the mountain   164
For the downward road is crowded   126
Forgive a lovelorn one this ardent suit   156
Friend of mine, come in to dine   124

From the Norse air to the loam   12
Fusion of Horizons   91
The Green Chapel   160
The Grey Havens   12
Haruspex of Paradox   79
Hazel Forks   59
He trilled like a bird on his day of arrival   144
Hexen in the Anticyclone   19
The Hidden Sin   74
Honour Song   112
How can I ever know you?   49
Hurricane Brown   110
Hymn of Welcome   157
Hyperboreans   37
I dreamed a dream and a scurvy dream   69
I feel the language in things   22
I Fell in Love   32
I fell in love with the roll of her drum   32
I must be going, no longer staying   51
I swore to mend your restless edges   120
I Went Hunting   24
I went hunting in the morning, Polly   24
Ice Age   5
If I was a pine I would ooze tar and shine in the moonlight   54
If There Is Any Light   108
If wisdom or idiocy send you adventuring   122
In Dispraise of Hunger   118
In January as it befell   148
In the dimming of the day   138
In the frozen ground, turnips rot   11
Is it not about time that the stars aligned?   5
It fell upon a Lammas eve   85
It was all around the time of the final Embertide   142
It's a country of absence and lack   108
It's of an untrue womb I sing   52
A Keen   144
Laden with a jaded soul   157
The Language in Things   22
The Last House   20
The Laverock in the Blackthorn   93
Learning Is Eternal   154
Light the need-fire, o light the need-fire   76
Lorica   166

Love is a fusion of horizons   91
May the horny-handed carpenter   103
The Merry Wake   88
The Mossy Shrine   114
My heart was waiting on the frontier   114
Ned Ludd's Rant (For a World Rebarbarised)   69
Never wrong a blacksmith   105
No Dawn Song   134
Now after Lammas there comes a harvest   118
Now the hinges of the year   37
O, I know she rose early for I heard her sweet singing   28
O, my girl of the old Armenian plain   7
O, the burning sand and the rolling wave   162
O, where is my own true love taken?   20
The Old Men of the Shells   45
One year I ran and ran and ran   56
Or would you trifle your life away   152
Orison of Union   162
Our masters distract us with catches and glees   150
Pangs   124
Peacock Strut   99
Plaint of Lapwing   101
Polly, you can tame the wild beasts   30
Raise me high, raise me high   26
Remembrancer's Blues   169
Riddle Me This   39
Ride the road with me, with me   110
River Rhine   43
Roomful of Relics   121
The Sacred Nine and the Primal Horde   76
Scarce of Fishing   140
Seagulls, Belts   7
Second Perthshire House Song   14
Show me the power that man cannot harness   39
Sing no dawn song, sing no dawn song   134
Slowly Growing Old   34
So Bored Was I (Dark Triad)   67
Son, you were weaned on the wormwood   132
Song Composed in December   82
Song of the Marvels   97
The Stranger with the Scythe   152
Tangled Hair   11
Tell me the marvels you saw on your rambles   97

The Tender Hour   156
The bothy is well lit tonight   13
The evening is growing dim   35
The fiend was reared in wonder-lock's embrace   79
The Flyting of Grief and Joy (Eternal Return)   64
The heaving ocean, so scarce of fishing   140
The hidden sin is half forgiven   74
The men have withdrawn and left me alone   121
The tides obey a lunar armoury   19
Then there came travellers, travellers three   99
This song's made in anger, this song's made in love   82
This Uneven Thing   120
Under No Enchantment (But My Own)   71
The Undiscovered Land   164
The Untrue Womb   52
Unyoked Oxen Turn   56
Vespers Chime   138
Waxwing   41
Waxwing, waxwing, what do you bring   41
Well, I startled a deer in the wood   136
Well, I'm singing an honour song for a never-born brother   112
Well, it's eighteen years since the loud cicadas   64
Well Lit Tonight (First Perthshire House Song)   13
What are you doing, soldier bold?   34
What cares the crow for the plaint of lapwing?   101
What god alive would scheme and strive   129
When first I awakened, the days they were straitened   168
When morning comes and we arise   116
When rain pours down to waken   93
When the sun is out   17
When you were on your Provincetown exile   9
Where does the River Rhine rise?   43
Where Twines the Path   47
Wheresoever twines the path, I will follow   47
The Whole House is Singing   28
Who'll mourn the warmonger when the warmonger dies?   169
Will you come to the merry wake, my bonny lassie?   88
Willie chose to walk abroad   95
Wormwood and Gall   132
The Wronged Blacksmith   105
The Yarn Unraveller   62
You look as good   3
Your family is haughty   62